This little church

WENT TO MARKET

The Church in the Age of Entertainment

Dr. Gary E. Gilley

 EVANGELICAL PRESS

EVANGELICAL PRESS
Faverdale North Industrial Estate, Darlington, DL3 0PH
England

Evangelical Press USA
PO Box 825, Webster, NY 14580

e-mail: sales@evangelicalpress.org

web: http://www.evangelicalpress.org

First published 2002 (Xulon Press; ISBN 1 5916 0049 9)
This revised and updated edition 2005

British Library Cataloguing in Publication Data available

ISBN 0 85234 596 8

All Scripture quotations, unless otherwise indicated, are taken from the New American Standard Bible, copyright © 1960, 1962, 1963, 1968, 1971, 1972, 1973, 1975, 1977 by the Lockman Foundation.

Printed in the United States of America

This Little Church Went to Market

To the faithful congregation of Southern View Chapel,
for allowing me to serve them for over 30 years

Contents

Introduction 9

1. A New Kind of Church 15

I. FORCES THAT ARE CHANGING THE CHURCH

2. Entertainment 23
3. Market-Driven Philosophy 33
4. Psychology 47

II. THE CHURCH THAT HARRY BUILT

5. A Church Losing Its Foundation 59
6. A Church Losing Its Message 67
7. A Church Focused On The Wrong Need 77
8. A Church That Misunderstands Worship:
How Shall We Then Preach? 83
9. A Church That Misunderstands Worship:
How Shall We Then Sing? 93
10. The Gospel According To Warren 105
11. A Church At The Crossroad 115

Appendix:
Repentance 119

Notes 135

Introduction

It had been years since I had seen Robert and Jennie Snodgrass, but there they were at the back of the restaurant where I was eating lunch with a few friends. Since it is God who looks at the heart and we, mere humans, at the outward appearance, I will admit that the first thought that crossed my mind, as superficial as that thought may have been, was that Robert and his wife had packed on a few pounds over the years. Actually, if the truth were told, the Snodgrasses had become downright plump.

This little encounter would be relegated to the 'so-what' dumpster except for one little detail: Robert and Jennie had been involved for a number of years in their own small business. Not just any small business, mind you; they were peddling a brand of diet pills which claimed to burn up all the fat from the food people ate. The promo promised their product would allow anyone to eat anything, in any amount, and not gain weight. And here were the Snodgrasses as supposed living proof, exhibit 'A'. Robert and Jennie, with protruding stomachs and rhino haunches, would visit in the home of potential clients, singing the praises of this miracle pill which had marvelously allowed them to become the slim and fit specimens that they are today. Yet, this is not the incredible part. What is really amazing is this couple did fairly well selling their anti-fat pills. Apparently, if you tell people with a straight face that you are 'Skinny Minnie' a certain percentage won't notice you can't button your pants.

Now, it is not my purpose in this book to pick on the diet industry, someone should, but not me. No, the subject in the crosshairs of my sight is the church of Jesus Christ. Don't get me wrong, I love the church and have dedicated my life to ministry within her. Parachurch organisations have their place on the Christian battlefield, but the church is on the front lines, where the real action is. It is for this reason I have pastored for over thirty years, never seriously contemplating any other ministry. I love the church. But the church, 'she is a-changing.'

Before I am misunderstood, I should inform you that I am not against change. Change is a natural part of life and a natural part of the church. However, there is a danger, I fear, of so changing the church that the church ceases to be the church. Like my chubby friends, the Snodgrasses, who loudly proclaim themselves to be thin when they are not, so the church may be in danger of false advertising. Even more importantly, it is becoming increasingly apparent that Christians are buying into these false claims, in spite of the evidence. Let me explain what I mean.

The Bible tells us that the church is the body of Christ (e.g. 1 Cor. 12). When we speak of the universal church, we are speaking of an organism consisting of all the redeemed throughout the church age, both living and dead. But the church does not function in universal fashion; it functions through particular assemblies, comprised of true believers, scattered throughout the world. Most references to the church in the New Testament are to local churches (e.g., the seven churches of Asia as found in Rev. 2 and 3).

Why did these local churches exist? What was their function? It is hard to improve on the pattern set by the very first church at Jerusalem. Acts 2:41-42 gives the details: 'So then, those who had received his word were baptized and there were added that day about three thousand souls. And they were continually devoting themselves to the apostles' teaching and to fellowship, to the breaking of bread and to prayer.' We see from these verses the essential functions of the local assembly: evangelism, instruction in the Word, participation in the ordinances, prayer and fellowship. Intertwined within these would be worship and edification. These activities defined the New Testament church, and distinguished it from a social club or a political rally.

Start with evangelism. Evangelism was the one biblically mandated function in which believers engaged outside of the assembled church. They did not invite friends to the church gatherings to win them to Christ. The church services were not geared for the unbelievers but for the saints. The closest we get to evangelism when the church is gathered is 1 Corinthians 14:22-25, which reads in part, 'If all prophesy, and an unbeliever or an ungifted man enters, he is convicted by all...So he will fall on his face and worship God.' Paul never tells us to target our church services toward the unbeliever, 'but if one should enter they should be impressed that God is certainly among you.' However, while the emphasis of the church gathered should not be on evangelism, the focus of the church scattered should be. As members of the body of Christ live out their lives in the world they should always be 'ready to make a defense to everyone who asks you to give an account for the hope that is in you' (1 Pet. 3:15).

Next, we note that when the early church came together, rather than spending the bulk of its time evangelizing, it focused on the apostles' teaching, or New Testament theology. They did this in order that believers might be able to grow in their Christian experience. The primitive church took this charge seriously. It was not enough to produce baby Christians; believers needed to be trained in the Word so they could move on to maturity (see Heb. 5:11-14). It was one of the primary functions of the local church to aid in this maturing process, for as Paul reminded Timothy the church was 'the very pillar and support of the truth' (1 Tim. 3:15). If the church is the dispenser of truth to both the lost and the redeemed, then dissemination of truth must be at the top of the church's agenda.

The early church also worshipped, prayed, partook of the Lord's Supper, and fellowshipped. These were the things that were important in the first church, and these are the things that should be important to us now.

To borrow from Dickens, as we move into the twenty-first century we may be living in the best of times and in the worst of times. The evangelical church is floating on a sea of success. Churches are growing, new buildings are popping up all over the place, organisations such as the Willow Creek Association are teaching us how to attract unbelievers to our services and to our message, and a mega-church is born every few days. Add to this the impact of movements like Promise Keepers and books such as *The Prayer of Jabez*, and it would seem that Christian leaders ought to be doing back flips of joy — this is certainly the best of times.

But something does not seem right. Someone has said they have no fear the church will not succeed, but that it will succeed in those things that do not matter.[1] Upon closer examination of evangelical churches across the world, especially the so-called market-driven variety, the careful observer notices a number of alarming issues. Success is everywhere, yet if we analyze the essential biblical components and functions of the local church, as identified above, warning flags are everywhere. Evangelism is one example. The market-driven church places great emphasis on bringing the un-saved to Christ (the Willow Creekers call them 'unchurched Harry and Mary'). But herein lays a problem. In order to evangelize we must first know the gospel. What happens when the church no longer knows the gospel, when it has co-mingled the gospel with pop-psychology to such an extent that the Apostle Paul would not even recognize it? Can unchurched Harry be saved through such a presentation of the gospel? Is it possible, as a result of this confused gospel, that the evangelical church is being flooded with churched 'Harry and Mary' who are nevertheless still unredeemed? If such evangelism has become popular on a wide scale, what does it tell us about the state of the church today?

If the church is the pillar and support of the truth and the children of God grow as the truth of God's Word penetrates their hearts, what happens when the church no longer knows the truth? What happens if it has confused the infallible truth of God with the philosophies and fads of the moment? If it could be demonstrated that humanistic and post-modern philosophies and the mindset of the age had replaced the careful, systematic study of the Word of God, what would that tell us about the state of the church today? If the elements of fellowship, communion, prayer and worship have always been an integral part of the local church, what happens when these activities are confused with, or diluted by, entertainment? If it could be demonstrated that what many call 'worship' is really amusement, what would that tell us about the state of the church today?

What we are anxious to discern is whether or not the emperor is wearing any clothes. You might remember an old story in which an emperor was duped into thinking he was wearing a beautiful new robe when in reality he was wearing nothing at all. The amazing thing was that since both the emperor and the people were told he had on a beautiful robe they all believed it must be so. This was reinforced when the tailors said that only foolish people would be unable to see the robe — and none wanted to be thought of as a fool. All went well until one untutored child cried, 'The emperor is naked'; everyone suddenly noticed, and all were duly embarrassed, even though, according to the story, the emperor continued the charade.

I fear the church is facing somewhat the same predicament. The most successful arm of the evangelical church in recent years, in terms of growth, money and prestige, has been the market-driven (seeker-sensitive, new-paradigm, user-friendly) church. Because of this success these churches are being mimicked all over the country, and indeed, the world. But is this church fully dressed? Is she outfitted in the biblically prescribed robes of evangelism, edification, worship and instruction? Or, is she wrapped in rags composed of empty human philosophy stitched together with bits and pieces of truth? If the latter is true, why have so few seemed to notice? It is the intent of this book to attempt to answer some of these questions.

1

A New Kind of Church

At the first tee, with great optimism and hope, I take a mighty cut at my Top Flite #2. I eagerly look up, fully expecting to watch that little white ball soar 250 yards straight up the fairway, only to find I have hooked it into the woods on the left. Determined not to repeat such an 'uncharacteristic' performance, I correct my swing a bit at the second tee only to slice the ball into the water on the right. By the third hole, I'm sure, I have all the bugs worked out. Taking a swing Tiger Woods would envy and that blows leaves off trees fifty yards away, I am amazed to find I have topped the ball, causing it to dribble harmlessly to the ladies' tee about twenty-five yards away. Frustrated, fully humbled, and deciding that keeping score would be a bad idea this round, I slump to the next tee. With no expectations and few hopes I leisurely drive the ball. To my utter amazement it is straight and long. Ah, I am back to form, I surmise. I am myself again — until the next shot. Oh, the joy of golf. And I took this game up to relax!?

The church, as observed throughout its history, reminds me a lot of my golf swing. She is constantly going from one extreme to the next, over correcting, coming up short, searching, and frustrated. Occasionally she gets it right and drives one down the middle, but repeating that feat is rare and soon she is slicing again.

The church growth movement is a recent example. Having watched a large segment of the church become content with short yardage and lousy scores, some decided that there had to be a better way. The church was not penetrating society; she was not pulling in the masses; she was not making a significant impact for the gospel. It was not that the church leaders didn't care; it was, it seemed, they lacked the 'know-how', the tools, to effect change. The gospel was still 'the power of God for salvation' (Rom. 1:16), but it was being rejected out-of-hand by too many. What was needed, apparently, were new methods to reach the lost, new techniques to promote the church, new packages for the gospel message. People, we were told, were not rejecting the gospel or Christ; they were rejecting our out-of-date, unappetizing forms, philosophies, and methods.

It is these pronouncements that we want to examine together in the pages that follow. We will say up front that the church growth experts have gotten some things right. They are calling for excellence rather than shabbiness; aggressive evangelism rather than indifference; direction and purpose rather than aimlessness; innovation and creativity rather than traditionalism at any cost; dedication rather than slothfulness. In all of these things we commend them. On the other hand, much like my golf swing, they have over corrected in important areas. These areas demand careful probing and biblical realignment.

While we will study the writings of various individuals who speak for the market-driven movement, we will focus on the two flagship churches: Saddleback Valley Community Church in Orange County, California, and Willow Creek Community Church, near Chicago, Illinois. These churches serve as the models that are reshaping the way we 'do church' today. As a matter of fact, many refer to these churches as 'new-paradigm churches'. Churches all over the world, even those which would claim to reject the church growth movement, are imitating the methods and message promoted by Saddleback and the 'Creekers'. Others have written about church growth, but these two churches have made it work, and for their success they are idolized and adored by the modern evangelical community.

The new paradigm

There are numerous things about the market-driven church growth movement that are disturbing, and we will examine these in due time. However, at this point we need to ask some questions: What exactly is a market-driven or new-paradigm church? How do they work? How do they differ from more traditional churches? What are they doing right? Why are they growing? And what can we learn from them?

First, we must distinguish between mega-churches and new-paradigm churches. Mega-churches are defined as those with average worship attendance of 2000 or more, but these behemoth churches come in all shapes, stripes and forms. Some are centres of great preaching and teaching, some are charismatic, others are little more than social clubs. New-paradigm churches, on the other hand, are identified by a philosophy of ministry intentionally designed to effect numerical growth. In their church growth methodologies more attention is paid to market strategy, business techniques and demographics than to New Testament instruction. This is not a criticism at this point (although we will critique these tactics later), simply an observation. Read the leading literature from the pens of the church growth experts (e.g., *The Purpose Driven Church*, by Rick Warren of Saddleback; *A Step by Step Guide to Marketing the Church*, by George Barna and *Inside the Mind of Unchurched Harry and Mary*, by Lee Strobel) and you will find a plethora of marketing techniques and only passing references to the book of Acts (the divinely inspired church growth manual) or any other Scripture.

An interesting article of the type that shapes the new-paradigm system is found in *American Demographics* magazine, a secular magazine designed to help businesses understand the consumer.[1] Several statements from the article are worth quoting since *American Demographic* seems to have its finger on the pulse of Americans' wants and desires. According to this article people today claim they are:

> Into spirituality, not religion…Behind this shift is the search for an experiential faith, a religion of the heart, not the head. It's

a religious expression that downplays doctrine and dogma, and revels in direct experience of the divine — whether it's called the "Holy Spirit" or "cosmic consciousness" or the "true self." It is practical and personal, more about stress reduction than salvation, more therapeutic than theological. It's about feeling good, not being good. It's as much about the body as the soul...Some marketing gurus have begun calling it "the experience industry"[2]

'Congregates', the authors believe, 'care as much about a church's childcare services as its doctrinal purity, pay more attention to the style of music than the pastor's theological training.'[3] If these things are true, how should the church react? Church-marketing consultant Richard Southern encourages us to make:

an essential paradigm shift in the way church is done, putting the needs of potential customers before the needs of the institutional church. Baby boomers [the inevitable target of new paradigm churches] think of churches like they think of supermarkets, they want options, choices, and convenience... Numerous surveys show that Americans are as religious as ever — perhaps more than ever...But what is on the decline is Americans' loyalty to particular denominations or traditions...In 1958 only 1 in 25 Americans had left the religious denomination of their upbringing. Today, more than 1 in 2 have left or switched...Protestant megachurches have become the evangelical answer to Home Depot, marketing such services as worship, child care, a sports club, 12-step groups, and a guaranteed parking place.[4]

The natural outcome for church leaders, who pour over such literature, is that they begin to use 'computerized demographic studies and other sophisticated marketing techniques to fill their pews'.[5] And the good news (it seems) is that it does not matter what a given church believes, for 'anyone can learn these marketing and outreach techniques. You don't have to change your theology or your political stance.'[6]

Springing from this fountain of demographic 'truth' is a whole industry of experts ready to teach church marketing techniques.

One such expert is Christian A. Schwarz, who is the director of the Institute for Natural Church Development. Schwarz claims that between 1994 and 1996 his organisation conducted 'the most comprehensive research project about the causes of church growth that has ever been conducted in the Christian church...More than 1000 churches on all five continents took part in this study.'[7]

From this mountain of research Schwarz has observed eight characteristics of growing churches. These are empowering leadership, gift-oriented ministry, passionate spirituality, functional structures, inspiring worship, holistic small groups, need-oriented evangelism and loving relationships. Some of these qualities we will examine more closely later, but at this juncture there are two things that draw our interest. Schwarz claims these principles work in any type of church anywhere in the world, and secondly, that if all characteristics are present these principles *will work every time*. 'Every church in which each of the eight quality characteristics has reached a certain level...is a growing church. There is qualitative value — which can be shown in exact statistical terms — beyond which a church will always grow.'[8]

One quality especially important to today's growing churches is enthusiastic worship services. Schwarz asks his readers, 'Is the worship service an inspiring experience for those who attend it? It is this area that clearly separates growing from non-growing churches. People who attend inspiring worship services unanimously declare that the church service is — and for some Christians this is almost a heretical word — "fun"'[9]

Growing churches are creating an atmosphere, an environment of fun. So fun has replaced holiness as the church's goal. Having a good time has become the criterion of an excellent, growing church, since fun and entertainment is what consumers want. Yet Bible references encouraging churches to become havens of fun are, as one may suspect, lacking. John MacArthur observes, 'Many Christians have the misconception that to win the world to Christ we must first win the world's favor. If we can get the world to like us, they will embrace our Savior. That is the philosophy behind the user-friendly church movement.'[10]

Let's play 'Who Wants to Be a Millionaire'. For $500,000: which of these churches was a growing church in the book of

Revelation; the church at Laodicea (Rev. 3:14-22), which saw itself as rich and wealthy and in need of nothing or the church at Smyrna (Rev. 2:8-11), which was described as poor, in tribulation and facing great persecution? Need a 'lifeline' you say? Here you go: God said of the Laodicean church that he would spit them out of his mouth, but of the Smyrna church that they would receive the crown of life. Confusing, isn't it? The growing church did not please God, while the struggling one did. Apparently, the Sunday morning worship attendance is not the criteria God uses to judge the true effectiveness of a local church.

This is something worth pondering as we press on to examine some of the forces behind the rapid change that is apparent in the modern church. We will begin with entertainment, a subject which might surprise many; but I believe in many ways we cannot understand what is taking place in the modern church until we have some comprehension of the powerful role entertainment has taken in our society today – and its impact on the people of God.

PART I

FORCES THAT ARE CHANGING THE CHURCH

2

Entertainment

When dealing with the subject of entertainment one is tempted immediately to consider the current trends facing our world. We are anxious to explore the place entertainment plays in our society, its encroachment upon the church, and its impact on the changing face of corporate worship. But to do so would not only be premature but also superficial. It is important first to lay a foundation upon which we can build and inspect. We need to travel down the road of the past to understand how we, as a society, got to the present. Having made that journey we would then be wise to take stock, consider precautions, and contemplate some adjustments. (All of this before we discuss entertainment in the context of the church.) If you will bear with me, this will not be a study of the Bible, but a study of our society — both past and present. Later in the book I hope to tie all of this together within a biblical framework.

Entertainment has a past

It would probably come as a shock to us who live in a culture in which entertainment (which we could define as activities designed to produce personal gratification and pleasure) has become the primary and most cherished value, to learn that it has not always been this way. One researcher discovered that the word 'fun' was of 'recent origin and that no other language had an exact equivalent to the English meaning, leading him to speculate that fun was neither readily understood nor fully accepted until the twentieth century. At the highest levels of culture it was taken for granted that good things were serious things.'[1] It is interesting to do a word study on the words 'laugh' and 'laughter', as found in the Bible. While these words are found a couple of dozen times, they are almost always used in a negative sense – usually of one who is expressing scorn or mockery (e.g. Ps. 2:4). Only three times is laughter portrayed as something clearly positive (Ps. 126:2, Prov. 14:13, Eccles. 3:4). Additionally, none of the great personalities of biblical times are ever said to have laughed as an expression of joy and happiness. Jesus wept, but we never hear of him laughing. The same is true of many others. This is not to say that godly people in biblical times never laughed, and the Bible is full of such terms as joy, gladness, rejoicing, etc., but for whatever reason, God did not see a need to tell us much about laughter.

As for the issue of fun, the Bible usually casts a pejorative connotation on the idea. The prodigal son no doubt had fun, as he squandered his wealth and his life, but then he came to his senses. But in fairness, when he came home his father threw him a great party where all but his brother rejoiced (Luke 15:32). Of course their joy was over a marvellous thing — the repentance of a sinner. We find a similar pattern throughout Scripture. The Old Testament Jewish feasts were unquestionably times of rejoicing, or at least that was their original intention. We find singing, fellowship, good food and drink, all in the context of worshipping and pleasing God. The joy wrapped around the feasts (and other happy events) was supposed to be centralized on God — he and his great provisions were to be the focus.

Solomon, on the other hand, gives us one of the few biblical pictures of a man chasing happiness and amusement in which he and his interests were centre stage — and it is not pretty. In the Book of Ecclesiastes, Solomon chronicles his journey in pursuit of something that would satisfy the gaping hole in his heart created by his abandonment of God. In his quest for pleasures, he ultimately did not find joy but increasing emptiness. When the laughter had died down he was still the same hollow man he was before. Solomon learned almost too late that while 'there is nothing wrong with entertainment…we all build castles in the air. The problems come when we try to live in them.'[2] The Bible, then, would not appear to condemn fun, laughter or entertainment, but would point us in the direction of examining both the focus and the motive behind such endeavours. For instance, the joy of the Lord is a common theme, especially in the Psalms. It is a joy centred on God, drawn from God's greatness, and focusing on God's glory. This is not exactly the typical concept of a 'good time' today.

Outside the biblical picture, and throughout the ages, until recently, certain worldly pleasures (such as drunkenness, orgies, immoral pursuits, sinful amusement) were seen for what they were – godless substitutes for the finer things in life. Nothing like the entertainment age, as we know it today, appears on the pages of history. Even during the days of the Roman Coliseum only a few were 'entertained'. The masses were excluded, or worse, executed.

Many have traced the roots of the entertainment explosion among the common people to radical changes taking place in Western society during the 1800s. No one has brought this to our attention better than Neil Postman in his excellent book, *Amusing Ourselves to Death*.

As these changes began to sweep across our land the intellectuals and cultural aristocrats were most often found sitting in their own corners, scoffing. For centuries the upper crust had an appreciation for the arts. But to enjoy the arts required a person to think, to meditate, and to engage the mind and the soul. This new brand of entertainment, increasingly being enjoyed by the masses, was mindless. It was 'about gratification rather than edification, indulgence rather than transcendence, reaction rather than contemplation, escape from moral instruction rather than submission to it.'[3]

In other words, the new forms of entertainment gaining popularity with the ordinary man were nothing more than senseless fun — and loved for just that reason. The elite hated entertainment for the same reasons that the working class delighted in it. The elite loved art, Shakespeare, excellent, thought-provoking literature and classical music while the masses were swooped off their feet by dime novels, ear-splitting music, and trash of all kinds.

Siding with the elite was the church, but for somewhat different reasons. The church had traditionally opposed amusement because its values and interests were in competition with those of organized religion — and because when a person was distracted by entertainment they could not focus on God.

But by the nineteenth century, the church, especially in America, had virtually no restraining effect on the new amusement juggernaut. There were two reasons for this. First, Americans simply did not go to church in great numbers in the nineteenth century. Many estimates place church membership at around 7 percent at the dawn of the nineteenth century and only 15 percent by 1850, after the so-called Second Great Awakening. Secondly, a dramatic shift had taken place in American forms of worship following the Revolutionary War. In the early decades of the 1700s churches and preachers were still under the influence of the Puritans. The primacy of the Word of God during this time was seen in the highly doctrinal sermons, which were addressed to *both* the heart and the mind. The plain-style worship services ensured that the focus was neither on the minister nor on the surroundings but on the God who addressed them in the Word. Language was used to evoke the awareness of the beauty of God's great and powerful redemptive love (just consider the sermons of Jonathan Edwards). Language was not used to entertain or fill church pews. Such unbiblical antics as Billy Sunday's 'sliding' into the pulpit and declaring 'safe by the blood of the Lamb' would have been disdained. Hymns were often 'lined out' (a method whereby the song leader read one line at a time, which the congregation would then sing then wait for the next line to be read), and sometimes eliminated altogether for fear that the people might be manipulated.

All that began to change in the 1740s at the time of the Great Awakening and the preaching of George Whitefield. When the embers of this time of revival died down, the church went into a drought. Church attendance began to dive, theology lost its appeal, the teachings of the Enlightenment began to catch on, and deism became popular. By 1800 the American church was in a dismal state and ripe for anything that would offer some kind of spiritual sustenance. The Second Great Awakening, which began in 1801 in Cane Ridge, Kentucky, would fill that void and forever change Christianity in America. Sermons of substance were rapidly replaced with emotional appeals. Doctrine was steadily replaced by 'conversion' stories, and the preacher's performance became more important than what was taught. Music took on a central role as emotionalism became the order of the day. Ministers began to study 'what worked' in order to draw a crowd. Charles Finney would perfect all of this in his *Revivals of Religion*, which changed the heart and soul of American Christianity. In other words, church services became a form of entertainment.

And so, when the amusement fad began to flourish in society, the church had little that it could say. Its biggest complaint would have to be that they were now in competition with secular forms of entertainment. While some voices decried Finney's 'new measures' (e.g. Asahel Nettleton), the church as a whole could not speak with authority against these amusements; it had lost its voice.

Fast forward

If someone had fallen asleep in 1850 and awakened a hundred years later, he would be just in time to watch society giving birth to the perfect entertainment transport — the television. Neil Postman argues persuasively that 'television has made entertainment itself the natural format for the representation of all experience…The problem is not that television presents us with entertaining subject matter but that all subject matter is presented as entertaining, which is another issue all together…Television is transforming our culture into one vast arena for show business.'[4] Television did not invent the entertainment age; it just perfected it.

The age of television ascended from the ashes of the age of exposition. In the 1700s and well into the 1800s almost everyone in America was a reader. 'America was as dominated by the printed word and an oratory based on the printed word as any society we know of.'[5] The outcome of such a state was a nation of people who could think, analyze, debate, formulate an argument, and understand and discuss issues, including theology. All of that began to change in the nineteenth century as entertainment started putting down roots in the lives of the American people.

Entertainment soon began to wrap its long tentacles around every aspect of American society. Not only was religion affected, but so were politics, the media, advertisement and life in general. Politicians today, I am certain you have noticed, no longer debate issues so much as they project an image, and why not for 'image is everything' according to the Canon commercials. And have you noticed how newspaper articles increasingly open like novels, setting the scene and attempting to draw interest. Education too has caught the wave. If kids would not listen to teachers and read books, maybe they would listen to puppets and watch cartoons. So the experts invented *Sesame Street*, and its clones, then soon thereafter began to praise its results.

Today kids also enjoy computer software, some of which has further metamorphosed learning into a game. But the long-term prognosis is not so bright, as our children are entering higher education and the adult work world with a game mentality. The consequence, educators are increasingly recognizing, is that we must make education fun and entertaining if we expect to keep the interest of our young adults. All that *Sesame Street* ultimately proved, as Neil Postman observes, is that children would love school 'only if school is like *Sesame Street*…As a television show *Sesame Street* does not encourage children to love school or anything about school. It encourages them to love television.'[6] And unfortunately, 'Television's primary contribution to educational philosophy is the idea that teaching and entertainment are inseparable…. [Which in turn] has refashioned the classroom into a place where both teaching and learning are intended to be vastly amusing activities.'[7] And when they are not, students become restless and detached.

Then consider advertising, which is as fine a mirror as you are likely to find for reflecting the values and reasoning ability of a society. Prior to the twentieth century advertisers assumed that consumers, since they were readers, were literate, rational and analytical. Therefore, products were promoted in rational ways – explaining their benefits – in order to entice a thinking society. That did not begin to change until the latter part of the 1800s when advertisers starting adopting jingles and slogans. The evolution of advertisement from that point would be an interesting study in itself, but even the casual observer today would note the almost complete lack of content in modern commercials. Increasingly, advertisement has almost no link whatsoever with the product. A commodity with redeeming value is not being sold — an image is. What this tells us about ourselves is that we have become people who no longer think and analyze; rather we respond to clever manipulation of our emotions.

Commercials no longer try to persuade consumers by appealing to factual information but by using emotions and images. The implications of this for the church should be self-evident. Postman suggests that 'the decline of a print-based epistemology and the accompanying rise of a television-based epistemology has had grave consequences for public life, that we are getting sillier by the minute.'[8] Another concerned author states, 'Entertainment reaches out to us where we are, puts on its show and then leaves us essentially unchanged, if a bit poorer in time and money. It does not (and usually does not claim to) offer us any new perspective on our lives.'[9]

It would appear, when it comes to entertainment, Christianity has caught up with the culture at large. One social observer, Neal Gabler, who has no axe to grind in this regard, making no pretence to be a Christian, has noticed, 'Evangelical Protestantism, which had begun as a kind of spiritual entertainment in the nineteenth century, only refined its techniques in the twentieth, especially after the advent of television. Televangelists like Oral Roberts and Jimmy Swaggart recast the old revival meeting as a television variety show, and Pat Robertson's *700 Club* was modelled after *The Tonight Show*, only the guests on this talk show weren't pitching a new movie or album; they were pitching salvation.'[10] Christianity on television, by necessity, has always been presented in the form of entertainment. Theology, rituals, sacred worship, prayer, and most other true components of the Christian faith, simply do not 'play' well on television.

As might be expected, the local church began to pay close attention. If they were to draw the masses, like the televangelists did, it apparently could best be done by wrapping the faith in the package of entertainment — for the people, having now been trained to be consumers, have also been taught that the ultimate sin is to be bored. Hence the birth of the market-driven church that caters to the insatiable appetite for amusement in society in general.

Overall there has been a great shift in what our culture values. One student of the times remarks,

> The old Puritan production oriented culture demanded and honoured what he called character, which was a function of one's moral fibre. The new consumption oriented culture, on the other hand, demanded and honoured what he called personality, which was a function of what one projected to others. It followed that the Puritan culture emphasized values like hard work, integrity and courage. The new culture of personality emphasized charm, fascination and likability.[11]

Steven Covey, in his widely popular book, *The Seven Habits of Highly Effective People* (many teachings of which I do not endorse), notices this same thing in his in-depth study of the 'success' literature published in the United States since 1776. He writes

> Almost all the literature in the first 150 years or so focused on what could be called the Character Ethic as the foundation of success – things like integrity, humility, fidelity, temperance, courage, justice, patience, industry, simplicity, modesty, and the Golden Rule…But shortly after World War I the basic view of success shifted from the *Character Ethic* to what we might call the *Personality Ethic*. Success became more a function of personality, of public image, of attitudes and behaviors, skills and techniques, that lubricate the processes of human interaction…The basic thrust was quick-fix influence techniques, power strategies, communication skills, and positive attitudes.[12]

It may be hard for us to imagine today, but right up until the end of the nineteenth century, the most important course in an American student's college career was moral philosophy, or today what we call 'ethics'. The course was seen as the crowning unit in the senior year, usually taught by the college president himself. As James Monroe, the fifth president of the United States, said of such classes, 'The question to be asked at the end of an educational step is not, "What has the student learned?" but "What has the student become?"'[13]

Today things are very different. We live in a society that increasingly drifts toward the form rather than the substance, which embraces the superficial, lives to play, will pay almost any amount of money to be amused, and prizes fun as the highest pursuit of life. Conviction has been replaced by thrill and few seem to notice. One cannot help but think of Pinocchio and his buddies on Pleasure Island. In the midst of mindless fun only Pinocchio seemed to understand that they were all being turned into donkeys.

One would hope that things would be different among Evangelical Christians, but such does not seem to be the case. It appears that the church is in lockstep with the world. The problem is this – Christians have been seduced and trained by the same forces that have enticed society as a whole. Too many Christians, just like their unsaved counterparts, are impressed by appearances rather than structure; are seeking thrills and excitement rather than substance; are more apt to respond to emotional manipulation than to rational discourse. How does a church compete in this rather crowded marketplace? If entertainment has become the standard way of life (as some are suggesting) then how can the churches vie unless they become a bastion of entertainment? But if it gives way to this powerful temptation has not the church been transformed into something other than the church? Postman, who does not pretend to be a Christian, nevertheless recognizes, 'Christianity is a demanding and serious religion. When it is delivered as easy and amusing, it is another kind of religion altogether…There is no doubt, in other words, that religion can be made entertaining. The question is, by doing so, do we destroy it.'[14] This is a question all serious Christians should contemplate. The problem is that the main business of entertainment is to please the crowd, but the main purpose of authentic Christianity is to please the Lord. Both the Bible and history have repeatedly shown that it is seldom possible to do both at the same time, for very long.

An antidote?

Is there an antidote for a culture being drained by laughter? I think not. When everything from politics to education to religion has become defined by its entertainment value, the culture as a whole seems to have become too trivialized to redeem, unless, of course, the Lord decides to intervene in a marvellous way. But there is an outside chance that God's people (at least some of them) can see through the smoke and come to different conclusions, and different ways of living. The key lies in the area of discernment. The author of Hebrews, addressing a whole different set of issues that had left his Christian audience immature and ineffective, called for this very thing. 'Solid food', he wrote, 'is for the mature, who because of practice have their senses trained to discern good from evil' (Heb. 5:14). There was no shortcut then, as there is none now, to maturity and discernment — solid food, in the form of in-depth study and application of the Word of God, is needed.

When Aldous Huxley wrote *Brave New World*, he certainly did not have biblical discernment in mind as the remedy for his envisioned societal ills. However, he did have a point to make that is worth considering. 'In the end, he was trying to tell us that what afflicted the people in *Brave New World* was not that they were laughing instead of thinking, but that they did not know what they were laughing about and why they had stopped thinking.'[15]

Christianity is designed by God to be a 'thinking' faith. If so, something appears to be seriously wrong. Os Guinness, for example, believes we are a generation that has 'dumbed down' everything that is important to the level of bumper stickers and greeting cards, and we are suffering the consequences.[16] One revealing bumper sticker, of the type Guinness has in mind, reads, 'There is no right or wrong – only fun or boring.' Yet, God desires his people to consider, reason, analyze and study. He has given us his Word in propositional form; a Word that must be carefully dissected if it is to be understood (2 Tim. 2:15). To allow ourselves to be pressed into the world's mould of entertainment without careful reflection based on the Bible is a terrible loss. God is not calling his people to a life of grumpiness, but surely if we, like the saints of biblical times, are looking for 'the city which has foundations, whose architect and builder is God' (Heb. 11:10), it will shape the way we live and enjoy our time on this earth.

3

Market-Driven Philosophy

The new-paradigm church has caught the wave of our times and has created a church for the entertainment age. Rather than expose and correct the superficiality and wrong mindedness of a generation addicted to fun, amusement and self, the modern church has all too often chosen to go with the flow and give 'them' what they want. To be sure they have camouflaged their product with religious words and Bible verses, but when the wrappings are removed it is very difficult to distinguish what the modern church is offering from what the secular world is offering. I intend to provide evidence for these rather caustic accusations in the chapters that follow, but first I must attempt to define exactly what kind of church I have in mind. Trying to identify new-paradigm churches, as far as doctrine or denomination is concerned, is like trying to nail Jell-O to the wall — it is a slippery proposition at best, and may be impossible. They must be identified on the basis of philosophy of ministry and church growth, rather than by what they believe doctrinally. Setting the agenda for new-paradigm churches is Willow Creek and its quasi-denomination, the Willow Creek Association (WCA).

The WCA is a loose association of hundreds of churches that have shown an interest in the method and philosophy of church growth as espoused by Willow Creek Community Church. While all members of WCA claim to be evangelical, they are as diverse as Presbyterian, Lutheran, Baptist, Methodist and Pentecostal.

In many communities, both evangelical and liberal churches are members of the WCA.

Much, at least at first glance, appears to be right about this approach to 'doing church'. After all, a lot of people seem to be getting saved and they're really 'packing them in'. Rick Warren puts a positive spin on new-paradigm philosophy in his very popular book *The Purpose-Driven Church*. Describing the ministry of Saddleback Valley Community Church, Warren ably demonstrates that many church growth principles are simply common sense on the one hand and purposeful, aggressive leadership on the other. Many of Warren's suggestions are excellent. Churches should pay attention to cleanliness and attractiveness, where people are going to park and how new people are going to feel walking through the doors. We should strive for excellence and do our best to communicate God's truth. And we should want to grow — in the right ways. Warren states, 'Every church needs to grow warmer through fellowship, deeper through discipleship, stronger through worship, broader through ministry, and larger through evangelism.'[1]

Who could argue with that? And who would debate the need for churches to know why they exist (their purpose), channelling their energies in that direction rather than wandering aimlessly as many do? And what about evangelism? Warren and the new-paradigm churches are geared to reaching the lost. While many churches are wasting precious energy fussing over the colour of the drapes in the foyer, the Saddlebacks and Willow Creeks are focusing their attention on bringing unchurched Harry and Saddleback Sam to Christ. You can't help but admire that kind of emphasis. To this end, Willow Creek, as much as anyone, has made it a passion to understand the unsaved around them (unchurched Harry and Mary) in order to more effectively communicate the gospel.

Willow Creekers know Harry's interests and passions, his goals and his hang-ups. They understand how his mind works and are doing all they can to make Christianity relevant. Churches that are growing are doing so primarily because they are focusing attention on the lost and visitors. They are churches that have not become in-grown and comfortable. None of these things are wrong; the problems are in the details. Having detoured around the Bible, the new-paradigm churches often look to other sources to develop their systems. Perhaps no single source carries as much weight in the 'seeker-sensitive' church as George Barna and his Barna Research Group. Barna, the evangelical counterpart to George Gallup, has ignited a number of fires in Christian circles with books such as *The Frog in the Kettle* and *Marketing the Church*. In his book *The Step by Step Guide to Church Marketing, Breaking Ground for the Harvest*, Barna declared that he and his adherents have won the ideological battle over the issue of marketing the church.[2] That is, only a few old-fashioned stick-in-the-muds still question the validity of the market-driven strategy.

Barna defines marketing as 'a broad term that encompasses all the activities that lead up to an exchange of equally valued goods between consenting parties.' In other words, 'activities such as advertising, public relations, strategic planning, audience research, product distribution, fund-raising and product pricing, developing a vision statement, and customer service are all elements of marketing. When these elements are combined in a transaction in which the parties involved exchange items of equivalent worth, the marketing act has been consummated.'[3]

Barna assures us that churches sell (or market) their product the same way that major retailers sell shoes and tools. But what is the church's product? What are we trying to peddle to consumers? This has to be thought through carefully, for unlike shoes and tools that have great attraction for some consumers, the gospel is repulsive and foolish to the unsaved. 1 Corinthians 1:18-23 is clear,

> For the word of the cross is to those who are perishing foolishness, but to us who are being saved, it is the power of God. For it is written, "I will destroy the wisdom of the wise, and the cleverness of the clever I will set aside." Where is the wise man? Where is the scribe? Where is the debater of this age? Has not God made foolish the wisdom of the world? For since in the wisdom of God the world through its wisdom did not come to know God, God was well-pleased through the foolishness of the message preached to save those who believe. For indeed Jews ask for signs, and Greeks search for wisdom; but we preach Christ crucified, to Jews a stumbling block, and to Gentiles foolishness, but to those who are the

called, both Jews and Greeks, Christ the power of God and
the wisdom of God.

How do we market a foolish, repulsive product? — By changing the wrapper, apparently. Note the subtle bait and switch in
Barna's philosophy, 'Ministry, in essence, has the same objective
as marketing — to meet people's needs. Christian ministry, by definition, meets people's real needs by providing them with biblical
solutions to their life circumstances.'[4]

At first glance most of us would be in agreement with Barna,
but look closer. By altering, ever so slightly, the biblical definition
of ministry, including the gospel message, as we will see, Barna
has made it attractive. If we can convince people that Christ died
to meet their needs, they will line up at our doors to buy our product. But is this the gospel message? Has Barna merely repackaged,
prettied up, the gospel 'product' or has he gutted it of its purpose
and value? This is an important question upon which so much
hinges — a question worthy of much consideration. As we will see
the market philosophy behind the modern church necessitates a
mutation of the gospel message.

Marketing the church

David Wells bemoans the new-paradigm church, 'Much of it…is
replete with tricks, gadgets, gimmicks, and marketing ploys as it
shamelessly adapts itself to our emptied-out, blinded, postmodern
world…There is too little about it that bespeaks the holiness of God.
And without the vision for any reality of this holiness, the Gospel
becomes trivialized, life loses its depth, God becomes transformed
into a product to be sold, faith into a recreational activity to be
done, and the Church into a club for the like-minded.'[5] Damaging
accusations; are they true?

The standard rhetoric coming from new-paradigm churches is
that they teach the same message, the same gospel, as the more
traditional evangelical churches; they differ only in methodology
and philosophy of ministry. Lee Strobel (former Teaching Pastor at
Willow Creek Community Church, now with Saddleback) writes,

'Objections [to the market-driven church] generally relate to the method that's used to communicate the gospel, not the message itself, and consequently we're free to use our God-given creativity to present Christ's message in new ways that our target audience will connect with.'[6] This is simply not the case. While some of the methods may disturb us, it is their message that is of real concern. It is important to understand at this point that it is one thing to market the church; it is another to market the gospel. In this chapter we are dealing with the unfortunate fallout of marketing the church. In a subsequent chapter the far most devastating impact of marketing the gospel message will be examined more closely. But at this point we cannot avoid mentioning that while the new-paradigm churches have dressed their gospel in the gown of conservative evangelicalism, it is in reality a masquerade, a costume that disguises a gospel message that would have been unrecognizable only a few years ago. Even as we analyze the methodologies for which the new-paradigm churches have become famous: their market-driven strategies, it would be a mistake to get sidetracked by superficial differences between these churches and more traditional ones. The real issue is how this philosophy is changing both the message and the essence of the church. In other words, it is impossible to truly separate our methodology from our message, for to a large degree they hinge on one another.

Perhaps it is for this reason that some within the market-driven church cringe at being called such. They would rather be hailed 'purpose-driven' (see Rick Warren's influential book *The Purpose-Driven Church*), or 'seeker-sensitive' (a.k.a. Bill Hybels). But others such as George Barna (the most highly regarded marketing researcher in evangelicalism) pull no punches. In his books, Barna outlines for pastors who have not had the privilege of a graduate course in marketing just how it is to be done in the church.[7] As to the debate within evangelical circles concerning marketing, Barna declares it to be over and the marketing gurus have won.

If this is true (and as one visits churches all over the country from liberal to conservative and observes their mimicking of market-driven principles one would have to agree that Barna has a good case), what exactly has been won (or lost, depending upon one's view)?

At the very top of the list marketing philosophies result in the hollowing out of the gospel itself. Let's follow the reasoning behind this statement.

As we have already seen, Barna defines marketing as 'a broad term that encompasses all of the activities that lead to an exchange of equally valued goods between consenting parties.' Barna moves on to give supposed examples of marketing in the Bible, including examples of marketing the gospel.[8] Unfortunately, in order to support his marketing strategy from the Bible, he must twist its meaning. For instance, Barnabas is given as a model of a marketing strategizer. Barna writes, 'Barnabas successfully tackled a tough marketing or "PR" assignment when he overcame the early disciples' fear of Paul, convincing them he was no longer a persecutor of the church' (Acts 9:26-27).[9] Jesus also owed his fame to marketing, according to Barna, because word of mouth is 'the world's most effective advertising.'[10] By his definition, all proclamation of any Christian message is an act of marketing. His argument is that all churches market, but some do not know it; the new-paradigm churches simply have taken marketing to a new level. It would seem at first that Barna has established his case but the marketing philosophy is a very different approach from the methods found in the Bible to spread the good news.

Start with Barna's definition of marketing. Is the gospel marketable by this definition? Is the gospel the 'exchange of equally valued goods between consenting parties?' Let's see. The gospel is offered by grace (undeserved favour) and received by faith. In the exchange God gets us and we get him (equally valued goods?). In the exchange we receive the righteousness of Christ, and he takes our sins upon himself (equally valued goods?). The market process breaks down in its very definition when the 'product' is Christ.

But is Christ the product of the market-driven approach? Barna would say yes but note his explanation: 'Ministry, in essence, has the same objective as marketing: to meet people's needs. Christian ministry, by definition, meets people's real needs by providing them with biblical solutions to their life circumstances.'[11] Although not so stated, I am certain if questioned Barna would say we meet people's real needs by bringing them to Christ. It should be kept in mind that 'ministry' to the new-paradigm churches, which have most often become evangelistic centres, means their efforts to bring unchurched Harry or Mary to Christ. But is the purpose of the gospel to meet the felt-needs of people? Is that why Christ came? Is this our message? We strongly protest such an understanding of the gospel.

The gospel is not bringing people to Christ in order to meet their felt needs. *According to the Bible the gospel is the good news that lost sinners can be forgiven of their sins and receive the righteousness of Christ in exchange.* This is the real need of humanity, the need for which Christ died. The new-paradigm church would have no problem agreeing that Harry's true need is salvation from sin (although sin is often redefined). But they do not believe that Harry will respond to such a gospel unless we dress it up with other enticing offers. Felt needs is the porthole, they believe, through which Harry is reached in order that his true spiritual need is met. According to their marketing research Harry is not interested in truth;[12] therefore, he does not react well to 'Thus saith the Lord'.[13] And Harry is not interested in the future (including heaven);[14] therefore reaching him through concern for his eternal destiny is futile. What Harry is interested in is feeling better about himself. He is asking, 'What can help **me** deal with **my** pain?'[15] He is interested in '**his** marriage, **his** friendships, **his** career, **his** recovery from past pain and so on'[16] (emphasis mine). Unchurched Mary, for her part, is attracted to churches 'where women have access to leadership and influence'[17] (i.e. an egalitarian approach). If we are to reach this generation, we must then 'market' the gospel as something that works (i.e., relieves pain and provides happiness, fulfilment and good self-esteem).

The leaders of the market-driven church believe that 'the most effective messages for seekers are those that address their felt needs.'[18] However, this approach is not drawn from the Bible; it is drawn from market research and the latest in pop-psychology. No one denies that there are many benefits to the Christian life, but these benefits must not be confused with the gospel. The gospel is not about helping Harry feel better about himself and his circumstances; it is about his rebelliousness against a holy God who will ultimately condemn him to hell if he does not repent and trust in Christ for the forgiveness of his sins. The distinction between the market-driven approach and the biblical approach lies largely in understanding this fundamental difference.

Market evaluation

Given the obvious fact that market-driven methodology works (almost all of the biggest and fastest growing churches around the world have hopped aboard the market-driven train), and granted that most westerners are pragmatic people who worship at the feet of the goddess success, what serious flaws could be found in the movement? Besides the alteration of the gospel as described above there are a number of lesser issues to concern us.

Big is good, small is bad; or where have all the people gone?

Most churches are small. In America, for example, fifty percent of churches average fewer than 75 attendees on any given Sunday, and only 5 percent attract more than 350, according to Barna's surveys. These statistics are not denied; it's their interpretation that is in question. Church growth gurus use these figures to prove that the church has lost its edge — it is not making a significant impact on society. But is this the case? David Wells shares his thoughts,

> A century ago, in 1890…the average Protestant church had only 91.5 members, not all of whom would have been in attendance on any given Sunday; a century before that, in 1776, the average Methodist congregation had 75.7 members. It seems to be the case that our churches today are about the same size as they have always been, on average, and the supposition that we are now experiencing drastic shrinkage needs to be clearly justified before it can be allowed to become the premise for new and radical strategies.[19]

As a matter of fact, church attendance in 1937 averaged 41% of the population, whereas it was 42% in 1988,[20] leading Wells to comment, 'Barna's efforts to make megachurches the benchmark of normality and then to argue that churches of conventional size are failures is simply unwarranted and wrongheaded.'[21]

It doesn't take a mathematician to realize that if the percentage of Americans going to church has remained constant, yet mega-churches are popping up almost weekly, then the giant churches are largely being populated by folks funnelling in from small churches. Just as the major retailers are killing mom-and-pop department stores, chain restaurants and groceries are doing the same in their respected venues, and the Mall has demolished 'downtown', so the mega-churches are doing a number on the small church. But large does not necessarily mean better, and when all the numbers are tallied, overall church attendance (on a percentage basis) is not increasing despite the methods championed by these mega-churches.

Who needs God? We have a program!

We are certainly in danger of reductionism, but when enormous faith can be placed in the marketing methodology, little room is left, or needed, for faith in God. One of the most blatant examples of the self-sufficiency of marketing is the idea/concept that the salvation of souls has a price tag. Barna suggests that a church might set an objective to 'lead 50 baby busters to Christ this year, for under $5000 in program expenditures.'[22] It should be noted that Barna is not suggesting a program in which x number of baby busters will be exposed to the gospel; he is speaking of the salvation of souls, a Divine prerogative. So for $100 per head we can bring people to Christ (at least baby busters). The need for prayer and trust in a sovereign God becomes questionable when we can statistically figure what it costs to bring a soul to the Lord. In Barna's defence this 'souls/dollar' strategy is not new. Both Charles Finney and Billy Sunday could predict to the penny what it cost to win a soul; their cost however ran between $2 and $3 a head — quite a bargain as compared to today. But of course if we factor in inflation we can apparently still win a soul pretty inexpensively.

Or take the church-growth consultant who boldly claims that 'five to ten million baby boomers would be back in the fold within a month if churches adopted three simple changes: 1. Advertise 2. Let people know about 'product benefits' 3. Be nice to new people.'[23] The belief in the omnipotence of marketing techniques is changing the nature of the church.

Should the consumer be king?

The premise of all marketing is that the consumer must be pleased; he must be kept happy; he must be given what he needs, or has been programmed to think he needs, if we are to succeed. This premise works very well for say, McDonalds, but can it be adopted by the church? Certainly it can, but is not the church and more importantly, the gospel message, in danger of being distorted in the process? Listen to these words by Wells,

> The fact is that while we may be able to market the church, we cannot market Christ, the gospel, Christian character, or meaning in life. The church can offer handy childcare to weary parents, intellectual stimulation to the restless video generation, a feeling of family to the lonely and dispossessed – and, indeed, lots of people come to churches for these reasons. But neither Christ nor his truth can be marketed by appealing to consumer interest, because the premise of all marketing is that the consumer's need is sovereign, that the customer is always right and this is precisely what the gospel insists cannot be the case' (emphasis mine).[24]

Even the *New Yorker* sees a problem with today's audience-driven preaching: 'The preacher, instead of looking out upon the world, looks out upon public opinion, trying to find out what the public would like to hear. Then he tries his best to duplicate that, and bring his finished product into the marketplace in which others are trying to do the same. The public, turning to our culture to find out about the world, discovers there is nothing but its own reflection. The unexamined world, meanwhile, drifts blindly into the future.'[25]

What if the consumer changes?

The following two quotes are worthy of pondering: 'He who marries the spirit of the age soon becomes a widower'; 'To be always relevant, you have to say things which are eternal.'[26] What happens when the fickle consumer changes his interests, or develops new wants, as he inevitably will? Will today's cutting-edge pastor suddenly find himself stampeded by the herd tomorrow? In order to avoid such a tragedy must he keep his ear to the ground of modern marketing techniques? Will he become a slave to polls and surveys? And how does all of this affect his use of the Bible? We don't have to have a crystal ball to answer these questions; all we have to do is look behind us. The church has always fought, and too often lost, the battle with its age.

Parallels with today are plentiful. For example, the 'Downgrade Controversy' of Spurgeon's time ultimately led to the liberalization of many of the evangelical churches of England. In our own country we think back to the early nineteenth-century changes that came about through the revivalism movement, best known by some as Finneyism. Os Guinness sees this as an important precedent because, as in our time, the change was not 'so much from Calvinism to Arminianism as from theology to experience, from truth to technique, from elites to populism, and from an emphasis on "serving God" to an emphasis on "servicing the self" in serving God' (emphasis mine).[27] Some are still alive who experienced the great Fundamental/Modernist battle of the first half of the last century in which the big names of the church invited us to court the spirit of the age. The fad was so popular that almost every major denomination in America eventually married that spirit and moved away from biblical Christianity. It was at that point that new fundamentalist denominations, churches, schools, and associations were formed. Ironically, it is these very institutions that are now flirting with the spirit of our age. The results are predictable.

Origen, in the third century, taught that 'Christians are free to 'plunder the Egyptians' but forbidden to "set up a golden calf" from the spoils.'[28] Easily said, but as history has proven, almost impossible to implement.

Michael Horton summarizes things well, 'By the time we are finished, we have entirely transformed the communion of saints. We did not even have to officially jettison the Bible, as the modernists did earlier this century. We did not have to say that Scripture failed to provide answers for the modern world or speak to the real needs of contemporary men and women, as the liberals said. **All we had to do was to allow the world to define the church instead of allowing the Word to define it**' (emphasis mine).[29]

When we speak of marketing the church we are not referencing such things as advertising church events, excellence in programming, being kind to visitors, or providing ample parking. No one is arguing the importance and value of such things. Marketing, as practiced by the new-paradigm churches, goes much further because its focus is on what the consumer (unchurched Harry) wants and thinks he needs, rather than on what God wants and what he says Harry needs. In other words, market-driven churches are built upon the foundation of polls, surveys and the latest techniques instead of upon the Word of God.

In order to market a church to the unsaved consumer, he must be given what he wants. Since unsaved consumers do not desire God, or the things of God, they have to be enticed by something else. Thus the temptation arises for a church to change, or at least hide, who they are so that they appeal to unchurched Harry. Additionally, the church is tempted to alter its message to correspond with what Harry wants to hear and thinks he needs. The end result is a felt-need gospel that appeals to Harry's fallen nature in an effort to entice him to come to Christ, the ultimate felt-need supplier, so that he is fulfilled and feels better about himself.

But, 'Can churches really hide their identity without losing their religious character? Can the church view people as consumers without inevitably forgetting that they are sinners? Can the church promote the gospel as a product and not forget that those who buy it must repent? Can the church market itself and not forget that it does not belong to itself but to Christ? Can the church pursue success in the market place and not lose its biblical faithfulness?'[30] I believe the answers to these questions are self-evident.

4

Psychology

A. W. Tozer warned decades ago of a new wind blowing across the fields of the evangelical church,

> If I see aright, the cross of popular evangelicalism is not the cross of the New Testament. It is, rather, a new bright ornament upon the bosom of a self-assured and carnal Christianity. The old cross slew men; the new cross entertains them. The old cross condemned; the new cross amuses. The old cross destroyed confidence in the flesh; the new cross encourages it.

> — If only Tozer could see us now.

In this chapter we want to look at perhaps the strongest influence behind the change in both the message and methodology of the new paradigm church — the invasion of psychology and its focus on felt needs. What has happened, I believe, is that the evangelical church has become a reflector of our times rather than a revealer. Guinness properly warns, 'The problem is not that Christians have disappeared, but that Christian faith has become so deformed. Under the influence of modernity, we modern Christians are literally capable of winning the world while losing our own souls.'[1]

We are driven

Rick Warren has written the most popular book to date promoting the market-driven concept of evangelism and church growth. *The Purpose-Driven Church*, which admittedly has a considerable amount of practical and helpful advice, nevertheless is laced with a felt need philosophy which, in my opinion, undermines the value of the whole book. It is Warren's view that in order to reach the lost we must begin with their felt needs.[2] He writes, '[For] anybody can be won to Christ if you discover the key to his or her heart.'[3] In order to discover the felt needs of the Saddleback Valley citizens he orchestrated a community survey of the unchurched (much as Willow Creek had done years before).[4] Once those needs were discovered, a program was implemented to reach the community by offering Jesus Christ, the gospel, and the church as a means of fulfilling those needs. Warren is so committed to this approach that written into the bylaws of Saddleback is this sentence, 'This church exists to benefit the residents of the Saddleback Valley by providing for their spiritual, physical, emotional, intellectual and social needs.'[5]

In support of this philosophy Warren does a couple of things. First, he offers Jesus as a model for reaching the lost through the felt need porthole.[6] Unfortunately for Warren's position the passages he uses are misunderstood, misapplied, and simply do not teach that Jesus reached the lost through felt needs. Did Jesus heal the sick and raise the dead as Warren claims? He certainly did. Did he do so because he understood Maslow's 'Hierarchy of Needs', which teaches that more important needs (such as the spiritual) will not be of concern until more basic needs (such as physical comfort) are met? Not at all. By studying too much psychology and not enough Scripture Warren misses the whole point of Jesus' miracles — to serve as a sign of his divinity and messiahship (Luke 11:2-6). A closer look at Jesus' evangelism shows that he always quickly got to the heart of the real need of his audience — their sin which separated them from God (e.g. John 3; 4; Mark 10:17-31) — in contrast to loneliness, poor self-esteem, lack of fulfilment, etc. In his own defence Warren states, 'Beginning a message with people's felt needs is more than a marketing tool! It is based on the theological fact that God chooses to reveal Himself to man according to *our* needs.'[7] Warren scrambles to offer theological proof for this assertion but there is none. He has intertwined pop-psychology with just enough random verses of Scriptures to confuse many of his readers. The apostles, on the other hand, would be absolutely dumbfounded to find their 'God-centred' teachings twisted to make them so 'man-centred'.

This needs-oriented approach to the Christian life is so prevalent within the seeker-sensitive camp that the little jingle,

> Find a need and meet it, find a hurt and heal it' has become the unofficial motto. Os Guinness observes, 'Few would disagree that church-growth teaching represents a shift from the vertical dimension to the horizontal, from the theological to the practical, from the prophetic to the seeker-friendly, from the timeless to the relevant and contemporary, from the primacy of worship to the primacy of evangelism, and from the priority of Christian discipleship in all of life to the priority of spiritual ministries within the church. But what happens when the much-heralded new emphases are seen from the standpoint of the Scriptures to be quite simply wrong? And what happens if tomorrow's "need" is for what is overlooked today?[8]

Continuing with Guinness's line of questions we might ask: What are the new-paradigm churches really offering that is attracting great throngs of people? Is this offering the same old message (the biblical message) in a new format, or is it a mutation of the real thing? And if it proves to be a mutation, what effect is it having and will it have on the modern church?

Psychologized Harry

It is my contention the gospel message has been altered. In addition, I believe the means for progressive sanctification and biblical living have been shifted from the biblical to the therapeutic. If this is so, how has this happened? What has changed our message from a force to a farce? A large part of the answer lies in the almost wholesale embracing of psychology by the Christian community. In order to support my argument we need, at this point, a general overview of the basic teachings propping up psychology, and how those teachings differ from those of the Bible.

Psychology, which follows the medical model, wants us to believe that a great number of our emotional and mental problems are really illnesses (we must distinguish here between true physical injuries and diseases of the brain from sinful choices and actions that have caused emotional or mental discomfort and distress). These problems have come upon a person, just as the flu might, and therefore are not the individual's fault. Since the person cannot help himself he need take no responsibility for his actions and can look for someone or something else to blame. For example, a man with a bad temper may blame his anger on his abusive father. Rooted deep in his 'subconscious', he has been told, is a resentment and bitterness toward this father (which he may not even recognize) that is now being 'acted out' in his own temper tantrums. Unfortunately, the man does not know this. So, he attempts to curb his anger through prayer and Bible reading, but it does no good. What he needs is a psychological expert to uncover the root forces behind his behaviour. When he discovers that he is an angry man because of his father, he can blame his problems on dad and feel better about himself. Once all of this happens (which could take years) he will begin behaving better, or so the theory goes.

The biblical approach, however, is that our man is responsible for his own actions. While it is true that he may have copied or learned bad behaviour from his father, and while it is true that his past will affect his present, nevertheless, this is no excuse for sinful actions. It is not necessary for this man to understand all that has happened in his past, nor is it helpful for him to shift blame. He must take responsibility for his own actions, confess his sins and seek to change according to biblical principles.

The psychological understanding of human nature is so radically different from that of the Bible that it might be useful to mention several other fundamental differences between psychology and the Word of God:

Difference in focus

The Bible is God-centred. Psychology is man-centred. The Bible teaches that our purpose in life is to glorify God. Therefore, everything else is subject to that purpose. Psychology, being man-centred, has as its highest goal the happiness of the individual. This is the foundation for the current emphasis on felt need. If mankind's greatest goal is his own happiness, then all other things in life, including God, become means to secure that happiness. Psychology teaches that happiness cannot be obtained if one is lonely, lacking in self-esteem, unfulfilled, etc. Therefore, whatever can satisfy these so-called felt needs is a positive thing. But such pursuit shifts the focus of life from others (Phil. 2:1-4) and God (1 Cor. 10:31) to the 'all-important' self. This world-view is completely at odds with the biblical world-view. Since this is true, to offer God or salvation as the means whereby our felt needs are satisfied is a perversion of biblical teaching at best, and more likely a false gospel.

Difference in view of human nature

One of the gravest flaws of psychology is its anthropology. Psychology teaches that human nature is basically good, or at least neutral. The reason that people misbehave is because of outside forces (such as society or parents) that harm them. These forces must be understood, dealt with and/or eliminated in order that the struggling individual can find relief and hopefully change. The Bible teaches, however, that people misbehave because they are sinners with a flawed and depraved nature. Change is effected through repentance of sin, the power of the Holy Spirit, and the understanding of the Word of God. The difference between these two views is pivotal.

Difference in view of values

The Bible teaches absolutes. Psychology teaches relativism. In a psychologized world we can each live out our own personalized set of values, but we must never condemn the values of others. In a biblical world God defines truth and that which does not meet God's criteria for truth is false.

Difference in our source for answers

Psychology teaches that individuals have the answers to life within themselves; they just need help discovering these answers. The Bible says that the answers to life are found within its pages as revealed by God in Christ. Christ claims to be the only way, truth and life.

Difference in methodology

Most forms of psychology teach that the key to personal problems lies somewhere in our past. The Bible deals with us in the present. As a result, God can command us to stop being angry or anxious immediately, without looking for root causes founded in the past. The past, especially our reactions to it, may have shaped what we are today, but change lies in the present as we choose to live obediently to Christ.

Psychologized Larry

In light of the above comments it might seem odd that Christians have taken such an interest in psychology, but they have. *Christianity Today* says, 'Right now evangelicals are swimming in psychology like a bird dog in a lake; they hardly seem to realize how much has changed (in Christianity over the last thirty years). They certainly do not feel in danger. But there is danger.'[9] Christianity and psychology both deal with the issue of how to live; yet, they come at it from opposing angles, draw different conclusions, and basically are not compatible.

So why has psychology had such an influence upon Christianity in the last thirty years? We might suggest several reasons.

First, Satan is always busy attempting to undermine the authority of God's Word. The first recorded temptation in the Garden of Eden was to doubt the Word of God (Gen. 3:1), and this has been Satan's focus ever since. Today, virtually every heresy found in the Christian ranks can be traced back to some form of rejection of the Bible as God's final authority. It may be pragmatism (which adds success to the Bible); mysticism (which adds experience); tradition (which adds the past); legalism (which adds man's rules); or philosophy such as psychology (which adds man's wisdom). The end result is all the same: the Word of God takes a back seat to the inventions and imaginations of men.

Secondly, there is very little understanding or desire for biblical truth and theology even among Christians. The Bible is not being expounded in many pulpits today. Christian radio saturates the airwaves with talk shows and psychology experts. Christian magazines aimed at the laymen are full of testimonies but devoid of solid spiritual food, and so few believers study the Word for themselves. As a result, we are a spiritually starved people who are no longer able to discern truth from error. So, when an appealing error such as psychology rears its head, we are all too ready to accept it as being from God.

Thirdly, seemingly good and respected Christian institutions and leaders support a Bible/psychology blend. Some of our finest seminaries, Bible schools, and mission organisations promote so-called Christian psychology. Numerous parachurch organisations have sprung up with the primary purpose of spreading this error. Is it any wonder that the average believer is perplexed?

Finally, there is confusion over the concept of 'All truth is God's truth.' This has become the battle cry of those who wish to integrate psychology and the Bible. The idea runs like this: God is the author of all truth, therefore, whenever truth is discovered we can be sure that it is from God. If mathematical and scientific truth can be discovered apart from the Word of God, why can't psychological truth be found and accepted in the same way? In reply we could make several observations: First, we must be careful how we define truth. Guinness says that 'in the biblical view, truth is that which is ultimately, finally, and absolutely real, or "the way it is," and therefore is utterly trustworthy and dependable, being grounded and anchored in God's own reality and truthfulness.'[10]

It is worth noting that Jesus claimed to be 'the truth' (John 14:6). Secondly, apart from the verification of God's Word the observations of mankind can never be proven as 'true'. For example, it would come as no surprise if many of today's medical and scientific 'facts' or 'truths' prove to be wrong in the future. To place the observations of mankind, in any field, on par with God's truth is a mistake. Infallible truth, in this life, is found only in the Bible. Finally, the Bible makes no claim to be a textbook on math, medicine or science. It does not explain electricity, detail the components of a balanced diet, give much insight into the need for sleep and exercise. When it speaks on these issues it is accurate, but these things are not its focus. The Bible does, however, claim to be a textbook on living, the same claim made by psychology; it declares itself to be able to equip us to live life in such a way as to please God (2 Tim. 3:16-17; 2 Pet. 1:3). To imply that the Word of God is inadequate to teach us how to live in this world is to deny its power and sufficiency.

What is the biblical counterpart to a psychologized approach to living? In passages such as Galatians 5:19-21, Colossians 3:5,8,9 and 2 Timothy 3:2-7 the characteristics of spiritual immaturity are identified. Here God tells us that we should expect people not living according to his truth to be unstable and easily deceived, guilty, selfish, and divisive. It should be expected that they will love wrong things, gossip, lack self-control, be angry at life, liars and deceivers, etc. However, to live this way will result in a host of what many today call emotional and psychological problems. If people are enslaved to such sins, why should it surprise us that they feel unloved, paranoid, anxious, burnt-out, hateful, depressed, empty and so forth?

The problems that people face today are real, and the psychological world often recognizes this fact. However, based on a faulty anthropology, as well as a misconception of truth and its source, psychologists will never discover the true origin of people's problems. Therefore, they cannot offer genuine, lasting help.

If we are to handle the problems that we face in a way that pleases God, we must grow spiritually (2 Pet. 1:5-8; Jas. 1:2-5) through obedience to the Word of God (Col. 3:16; Acts 20:32; 2 Tim. 3:16,17) as the Holy Spirit works in our lives (Gal. 5:16, 22-25; also see Heb. 5:12-14). This method of change and growth may sound simplistic and superficial to a world, and all too often a church, duped by psychological theories, but it is the biblically prescribed methodology and has been recognized as such by the evangelical church throughout history.

PART II

THE CHURCH THAT HARRY BUILT

5

A Church With The Wrong Foundation

My first encounter with the encroachment of psychology upon the church was my senior year of Bible college in 1972. As I prepared for the pastorate at a well-known Bible institute, I had been saturated in the study of Scripture and theology. As a senior I was required to take a course in 'pastoral counselling', which proved to be almost identical to a course in psychology that I had taken at the University of Virginia. That same year I was asked, along with several others, to be a registered assitant in the men's dorm. As part of our preparation we were given training in the latest rage in pop-psychology (which, by the way, has since been relegated to the psychological junk heap). At the time I remember my wide-eyed amazement that all my studies in Scripture apparently did not equip me to deal with the real problems that would face me in my future ministry. Bible study and theology were great for salvation and sanctification, but there apparently existed a set of problems and needs 'out there' that required more than the 'simplistic' solutions found in God's Word. The Bible, after all the dust had cleared, needed help from Freud. Unable and ill equipped to deal with my newfound knowledge, I tucked it away for safekeeping. Later, in the early days of pastoring, I decided to pursue a master's degree in psychology in order to help people with their 'real' problems. But it soon became abundantly clear that something was seriously wrong. Virtually everything that I learned in my psychology courses contradicted the Bible. So I ended my illustrious career as a would-be pastor-psychologist and went back to studying the Bible, which has proven itself more than adequate throughout the years for every need and concern that has come my way. Meanwhile, immersed in my own ministry and Bible study, I was somehow oblivious to psychology's hijacking of the evangelical church during the 1970s and 80s. One day I awoke, in sort of a Rip Van Winkle experience, to find that my world, the world of the church, had changed, and I had been 'left behind'. Where had everyone gone? Most churches were now talking about dysfunctional families, poor self-image, co-dependency, addictions, 12-step programs, and needs, lots and lots of needs that the church was supposed to meet. More Christians were obtaining their philosophy for living from popular talk-show hosts than from Jesus and Paul.

When Christian leaders saw this metamorphosis of God's people, a metamorphosis that they had helped create, they could pull in the reins, denounce this caricature of the Christian faith and repent of their part in its birth, or they could jump on the float and join the parade. Most, recognizing that this is what the people now wanted, what they expected, what they had been trained to 'need', chose the float approach. Give Christians the need-oriented pop-psychology that they had grown to love, they decided, just alter it a bit with some verses and some references to Jesus — they would never catch on that what they were swallowing was not biblical Christianity at all, but an almost unrecognizable perversion. Whether this approach was calculated or naively taken matters little. The result is the same: a psychologized Christian community which no longer recognizes the difference between the teachings of the Bible and the teachings of Carl Rogers and no longer cares.

Since the Christian was now indistinguishable in philosophy from the world, both having fallen in love with psychobabble, the offence of the cross became far less offensive. It was only a short step for someone (Robert Schuller is a worthy candidate as we will see) to develop a psychologized church for the already psychologized unchurched Harry (and churched Larry). This would be a church that would offer the same things to Harry that secular society offered, only better, since Jesus was better than Carl Rogers,

Oprah and Freud combined. And so it was — 'The new-paradigm churches, then, appear to be succeeding, not because they are offering an alternative to our modern culture, but because they are speaking with its voice, mimicking its moves.'[1]

A little history

The church growth movement owes much to Robert Schuller. He claims to be its founder, at least in this country, by being the first to launch the marketing approach in Christianity. 'The secret of winning unchurched people into the church', Schuller said, 'is really quite simple. Find out what would impress the nonchurched in your community [then give it to them].'[2] Believing that expository preaching is a waste of time, and borrowing the philosophy of his mentor Norman Vincent Peale, Schuller 'began to communicate a message of Christianity that focused on meeting the emotional and psychological needs of people.'[3] Schuller laid out his philosophy of ministry in his 1982 book *Self Esteem: The New Reformation,* in which he called for a radical shift in the church's focus from God to human needs. The most important issue before Schuller was to determine, through some means, the deepest human need upon which the church should focus. He decided that mankind's most fundamental need was self-esteem; a 'need' nowhere mentioned, alluded to or even hinted at in the Bible. He then went on to wrap his theology and church growth strategy around this all-important need. Originally Schuller's church growth philosophy met with scorn and denunciation by conservative Christians everywhere. But while Christian leaders held the theological front against need-oriented Christianity they were out-flanked by pragmatism. It just so happened that Schuller's methodology worked, and those who employed it were seeing exponential numerical growth in their churches. In most arenas truth doesn't stand a chance against success; this proved to be the case in the church growth wars.

If Robert Schuller was the architect of the user-friendly church, then Bill Hybels, pastor of Willow Creek Community church, became the contractor. Working from Schuller's premise that, as

Strobel would later communicate, 'The most effective messages for seekers are those that address their felt need',[4] it remained for Hybels and company to determine which felt-needs required most attention. Leading the pack, Hybels decided, was not self-esteem, as Schuller taught, although he did not reject it, but rather personal fulfilment (or the pursuit of happiness). This view was derived from secular psychology, not the Bible, as we demonstrated in our last chapter. Fulfilment was followed by identity, companionship, marriage, family, relief of stress, meaning and morality.[5] To Hybels, fulfilment was the felt need that encompassed and defined all others.

Since, to the founders of the new-paradigm church, felt needs are the driving force behind the actions and attitudes of people, and since Christianity, Hybels would argue, is the best means to solve problems and satisfy the desire for fulfilment,[6] he developed the gospel of personal fulfilment. According to the research book *Willow Creek Seeker Services* by G. A. Pritchard, the canon within the canon at Willow Creek is that human beings can be fulfilled. Fulfilment permeates *every* venue at Willow Creek, even leading to a redefinition of sin. 'Instead of only portraying sin as selfishness and a rebellion against God, Hybels also describes it as a flawed strategy to gain fulfilment.'[7]

It should be noted that while this felt need strategy is not derived from the Bible, coming clearly from secular psychology, it nevertheless has become the foundation of the new-paradigm church.

The repercussions

The result of psychology's invasion of our culture has been, as R. Albert Mohler Jr. noticed, 'Americans are now fanatic devotees of the cult of self-fulfilment and personal autonomy.'[8] The role of the church should be to challenge the spirit of the age, for as Wells points out, 'The church is in the business of truth, not profit.'[76] Unfortunately, 'The healers of our time – psychotherapists and advertisers – have extended their long reach into the life of the church as well. Our secular healers have populated the Church with their close cousins.'[9] Even the language of theology has been replaced by the vocabulary of the therapeutic.

These new cousins have affected every aspect of church life. Take worship for example — new-paradigm pastor Wes Dubin goes on the offensive when his entertainment oriented worship services are challenged. In his church he claims, 'It (worship) is not all gloom and doom, and all of us take our Bibles and just bore each other; let's show them that we can also have fun.'[10] There we have it again – the entertainment oriented church, the First Church of Fun. Certainly there is a time for fun in the church but surely, 'The purpose of worship is clearly to express the greatness of God and not simply to find inward release or, still less, amusement. Worship is theological rather than psychological.'[11]

And then there is this issue of sin. In a psychological world sin is reduced to sickness and addiction. The sinner is not seen as depraved, but as a victim. What is lost is our capacity to understand life, and ourselves, as sinful. When the seeker-sensitive church adopts the language and theology of psychology, it then attempts to dispense psychological prescriptions for life's issues rather than biblical ones, for after all, it reasons, the world now thinks within the framework of psychology and we must be relevant. Rather than challenge and confront the world's wisdom the modern church is seeking to sanctify it. The result is, as the prophet Jeremiah warned in his day, 'They have healed the brokenness of My people superficially' (Jer. 6:14).

The emphasis on psychology is also changing the focus of the church. Pritchard is right when he says, 'Instead of looking at God's face, this teaching suggests that individuals look in the distorted mirror of modern psychology.'[12] Pritchard claims that when he attended the church, the majority of the books sold in Willow Creek's bookstore were psychological and self-help books, with the decidedly anti-Christian *Codependent No More* by Melody Beattie the top seller.[13] This accent on psychology, 'instead of encouraging Creekers to know and love God, encourages them to know and accept themselves and develop a strong self-esteem. The goals and means of one's ethics change from a God-centered to a human-centered orientation…Willow Creek Christians have accepted the psychological framework as foundational to their self-understanding and as a trustworthy guide for daily living.'[14]

Pritchard's assessment of the psychological influence at Willow Creek is lethal: 'Ironically, while Hybels is evangelizing those in the world toward Christianity, he is also evangelizing Christians toward the world. As the unchurched Harrys in the audience (10 percent) move closer to Christianity, the Christians in the audience (90 percent) are often becoming more psychological and worldly…In the effort to become relevant Willow Creek ironically is in danger of becoming irrelevant.'[15] Pritchard's critique of the need-oriented approach to 'doing church' is worthy of quoting extensively:

> The unintended consequences of this approach are that Hybels incorporates large chunks of the American psychological worldview into his basic teaching and teaches that fulfillment is a consequence of the Christian life. There is a lack of critical evaluation to Willow Creek's approach to relevance. This felt-need approach to relevance ultimately distorts their Christianity.
>
> A more biblical approach to the current American fixation with fulfillment is to call it the idolatry that it is. Jesus does not guarantee that to follow Him will make one fulfilled. In fact, at several points, the direct opposite is communicated: 'I have chosen you out of the world. That is why the world hates you' (John 15:19); 'I did not come to bring peace but a sword' (Matthew 10:34); 'If they persecuted Me they will persecute you also' (John 15:20). The temptation to say that Christianity will meet all one's needs and provide fulfilment is not true to biblical Christianity.
>
> Willow Creek's unintended failures result from an uncritical use of various cultural tools and ideas (marketing, psychology, media). In particular, their mistakes are rooted in a superficial understanding of the American culture and an inadequate grasp of Christian theology.[16]

The faith of the ages

The seeker-sensitive experts would defend marketing as a tool they use to attract more unchurched Harrys to hear the gospel. 'Methods change, the message stays the same', is the cliché. What they do not seem to understand is that the message will ultimately be shaped by the method. This is especially true of marketing since it 'shapes how one views the world. People become "consumers" and "target audiences". These consumers have 'felt needs,' which "research" discovers in order to modify the "product" to meet these needs.'[17]

There exists an important difference between the New Testament church and the new-paradigm church. The church, the New Testament teaches, has as its aspiration the glorification of God and the training of his people concerning how to please him. In the process needs may very well be met but the primary purpose of the church is not to meet people's needs (except the need for righteousness). In the seeker-sensitive church, 'needs' reign supreme; God exists to meet Harry's needs. Harry comes to Christ, not to glorify him, but to find the promised fulfilment and happiness in this life. When Harry is attracted through a felt-need philosophy, he will not be retained when that approach is no longer used. In other words, if Harry is drawn to the church in order to *get*, in order to satisfy his flesh, he is not likely to stay around when and if he discovers that Christ calls for him to lose his life for Christ's sake (Matt. 16:25). The result is that churches which have been built on the quagmire of the superficial must remain superficial if they hope to retain their Harrys and Marys.

David Wells asked the right question of these seeker-sensitive churches, 'Does the church have the courage to become relevant by becoming biblical? Is it willing to break with the cultural habits of the time and propose something quite absurd, like recovering both the word and the meaning of sin?...I fear that the seeds of a full-blown liberalism have now been sown, and in the next generation they will surely come to maturity.'[18] I agree with the closing sentences in *Losing Our Virtue*, 'We need the faith of the ages, not the reconstructions of a therapeutically driven or commercially inspired faith. And we need it, not least, because without it our postmodern world will become starved for the Word of God.'[19]

6

A Church With The Wrong Message

Counterfeit money is recognized by those who know how to identify the real thing. Before we examine the gospel message found in the new-paradigm churches, it would be best to examine the gospel message found in the Bible. The good news in a nutshell is this: Harry (to use Willow Creek's name for the unsaved) is a sinner, in full-blown rebellion against God (Rom. 3:23; 5:1-12). While some Harrys are outwardly religious and some even desire the gifts and benefits that God can supply, no Harrys truly seek after God or desire him (Rom. 3:10-18). As a result of Harry's sinfulness he is under the wrath of God (Rom. 1:18), faces future judgment (Heb. 9:27), will die both physically and spiritually (Romans 6:23) and will spend eternity in hell (Rev. 20:11-15).

It is because of Harry's hopeless plight, and the fact that he can do nothing to redeem himself in God's eyes (Titus 3:5), that Jesus Christ, through grace alone, not because of Harry's value and worth (Eph. 2:8), became a man, died on the cross (Romans 5:8) thus taking Harry's sin upon himself and satisfying the wrath of God (Heb. 2:17), and resurrected from the dead, in order that Harry could be saved from his sin and be given the righteousness of Christ (Rom. 4). While all of this is a gift from God, Harry obtains that gift through the exercise of faith (Eph. 2:8,9) – purely taking God at his Word, trusting that God will save him if only he truly believes.

What I hope to demonstrate in this chapter is that while many within the seeker-sensitive movement would ascribe to most of the above definition for the gospel, this is not how the gospel is being presented to Harry. Rather Harry is being told that he is so valuable to God that he sent his Son to die for him. This is, in effect, a denial of grace, whereby God grants us undeserved favour. Harry is also being told that if he will come to Christ, Christ will meet all of his felt needs and that will lead to personal fulfilment. Harry is then being asked to trust in Christ, the great 'Needs-Meeter', who will end his search for a life of happiness and fulfilment.

This, I suggest, is not the gospel at all, but the 'Gospel of Me', the 'Gospel of Self-Fulfilment,' the 'New Gospel'. 'We must never confuse our desire for people to accept the gospel,' Oswald Chambers warned long ago, 'with creating a gospel that is acceptable to people.' 'How we define the problem will define our gospel. If the "big problem" in the universe is my lack of self-esteem, the gospel will be "finding the neat person inside of yourself". If the great question is "How can we fix society?" the gospel will be a set of moral agendas complete with a list of approved candidates. But how often do we discuss the "big problem" as defined by Scripture? That problem is the wrath of God.'[1]

Harry would come to church but...

The reason unchurched Harry is unchurched is, to the market-driven proponents, a matter of Harry being a fallen creature who has rejected God and has little, if any, attraction toward the things of God. Right? No, not at all. Rather, Harry would love to come to church, and ultimately receive Christ, if only the church would learn to market and present its product better. Lee Strobel has written a book entitled *Inside the Mind of Unchurched Harry and Mary,* in which he presents the definitive understanding of the gospel message as comprehended by the new-paradigm church. Strobel assures us that marketing studies have shown that 'Harry has rejected church, but that doesn't necessarily mean he has rejected God.'[2] Yet, the Bible clearly says that humanity does reject God (Rom. 3:10-18; 5:1-12; 1 Cor. 1:18ff). What surveys really show is that people do not reject gods of their own creation and imagination; but they do reject the true God.

What we supposedly learn from marketing study is that the real reason Harry doesn't come to church has little to do with his rebellious, God-rejecting nature. Rather it is because church is boring, predictable, irrelevant, money hungry,[3] and does not meet his needs.[4] The new-paradigm church operates under the credo that Harry is 'hostile to the church, friendly to Jesus Christ.'[5] They 'have the misconception that to win the world to Christ we must first win the world's favor. If we can get the world to like us, they will embrace our Savior. The expressed design of the user-friendly philosophy is to make unconverted sinners feel comfortable with the Christian message.'[6] The only way this is possible, I fear, is to change the message. For the gospel message is not a comfortable one for the unbeliever, and to try to make it so merely deforms it.

Reaching Harry with the gospel

It is clear, when one studies Scripture rather than marketing surveys that the seeker-sensitive gospel message is flawed at its roots — it has a faulty anthropology. It views Harry as attracted to and even friendly with God but turned off by the out-dated methods of the church. Once that premise is accepted, the methodologies of the user-friendly church are logical. All that remains is to discover what Harry wants in a church, and in a God, and give it to him in an attractive format. In other words, make him an offer he can't refuse. On the negative side we must understand that, according to Strobel, 'Unchurched Harry doesn't respond well to someone who predicates a command on, "Thus saith the Lord."'[7] Nor is the way to Harry's heart through the porthole of truth. For, again, Harry is a pragmatist; his question is does Christianity work?[8] Harry is also an existentialist; 'Experience – not evidence – is his mode of discovery.'[9]

If it is accepted that Harry is not motivated by the commands of God, nor is he all that interested in truth, the evangelist can abandon the direct approach. Further since Harry is looking for something that will help him reach his goals in life and to feel good in the process, it makes sense to embellish the gospel to draw his attention. The new-paradigm church does this by focusing on the gospel of felt need. 'The Church's problem today is simply that it does not believe that, without tinkering, the gospel will be all that interesting to modern people.'[10] And so tinker it must. There is a downside to all this tinkering, of course, a big one. As Guinness warns, 'Whereas both the Bible and the best thinkers of Christian history invite seekers to put their faith in God because the message conveying that invitation is true, countless Christians [or at least those who think they are] today believe for various other reasons. For instance, they believe faith is true "because it works" (pragmatism), because they "feel it is true in their experience" (subjectivism), because they sincerely believe it is "true for them" (relativism) and so on…For all of them the outcome is a sickly faith deprived of the rude vigor of truth.'[11]

The gospel of felt need

From psychology, Strobel and the seeker-sensitive church have discovered that both baby boomers and busters have learned to expect that their needs should be met, jobs would be provided, money would be available, and problems would be solved. The result is a generation of young adults who want and expect everything right away. Life is to be lived for the present. There is little awareness of a philosophy that says we should make long-range plans, or work hard today so things will be better tomorrow. This is a 'now' generation that has little interest in any religion that talks about sacrifices, heaven, or 'the sweet by-and-by.' They want to hear about a faith that works now and brings immediate results.[12]

If this is true, how are we to proclaim the gospel to a pampered, self-centred generation that demands society meets their every whim? Previous generations of Christian leaders, including biblical ones, would use these traits to point to evidence of sin in Harry's life. 'Look Harry,' they would have said, 'your selfish, proud heart reveals just how sinful and rebellious you really are.' They would have called Harry to repentance from such a lifestyle, and to faith in Christ for forgiveness of these very sins. Then they would have challenged new-believer Larry to abandon his self-centeredness, call for a life of self-sacrifice, humbly allowing the Spirit of God to transform him into Christ-likeness.

But the modern church sees it differently. Strobel writes, "Our challenge, then, is to help this new generation of unchurched Harrys understand that Christianity does work, that is, that the God of the Bible offers us supernatural wisdom and assistance in our struggles, difficulties, and recovery from past hurts."[13] Harry simply will not be attracted to Christ if we present him with the biblical gospel. We must then change the message in order to make it more palpable to this generation of ultra-self-centred Harrys and Marys. What worked at one time simply does not speak to today's Harry. David Wells has nailed down the prevailing attitude when he writes, 'What our culture suggests is that all of the greatest treasures of life are at hand, quite simply, in the self. Religious man was born to be saved, but psychological man was born to be pleased. "I believe" has been replaced by "I feel". The problem is that we have not been feeling so well recently.'[14]

There is just enough truth in Strobel's statement to throw most of us off guard. Does Christianity work? Does God offer wisdom and help during times of struggle? Certainly, but is this the gospel? Is the good news that Christ died for our sins in order to free us from the wrath of God and give us the righteousness of Christ; or is the good news that Christ died in order that we might feel better about ourselves and have our felt needs met? These are two separate gospels. It should concern us deeply that the apostle Paul soundly condemned those at the church of Galatia who attempted to modify the gospel to suit their tastes. He writes, 'But even though we, or an angel from heaven, should preach to you a gospel contrary to that which we have preached to you, let him be accursed' (Gal. 1:7). Solemn words that we dare not take lightly.

A few more quotes from Strobel's book will help identify exactly what the new-paradigm church is offering the unbeliever. '"We baby boomers aren't coming to church to become members," said one pastor, himself a boomer. "We are coming to *experience* something. Yes, even to *get* something."'[15] Strobel suggests that the best way to reach Harry and Mary with the gospel is to discover what it is that they want to 'get', what it is they want to experience; what is it they want to obtain in life, and offer it to them in Jesus. For example, 'If you discover that unchurched Harry suffers from a sagging self-esteem…you can tell him how your own self-esteem has soared ever since you learned how much you matter to God.'[16] Never mind that the concept of self-esteem is foreign to the Bible, even against it; never mind that the real issue that Harry struggles with, according to the Bible, is pride not low self-esteem; the gospel is now gift-wrapped to offer Harry what he has been conditioned to believe he needs.

Not everybody is in need of an ego boost however; some are looking for thrills, excitement, and adventure. Fortunately for the quick-minded evangelist the gospel resembles a chameleon, taking whatever shade is needed. Strobel assures such thrill-seekers that he 'learned that there is nothing more exciting, more challenging, and more adventure-packed than living as a devoted follower of Jesus Christ. What I found is that there's a big difference, between *thrills* and *thrills that fulfill.*'[17] So now Jesus Christ can be offered as the Big Thrill, the ultimate in excitement. Not only is this a mis-representation of Christ but it just does not square with the facts. I wonder how thrilled the saints described in Hebrews 11:36-38 were as they were mocked, beaten, put to death, and watched their children murdered, became homeless and lived in holes in the ground. The new-paradigm church is offering a purely com-mercialized, yuppie brand of Christianity found nowhere in the New Testament. As Wayne Jacobsen observes, 'Much of the gos-pel presented today befits less the God of the ages than a fairy god-mother – offering people by God's hand what they've been unable to achieve for themselves: wealth, fame, comfort, and security.'[18]

A serious question arises at this juncture. Is a person coming to Christ in order to bolster her self-esteem or experience a great thrill, truly born again? If Mary does not clearly understand that the real issue on the table is her personal sinfulness that has offended a holy and righteous God, does she understand the gospel at all? If she believes that Christ died on the cross to save her from a poor self-image in order to give her a fulfilling life brimming with excite-ment, has she not been presented with a gospel so hopelessly mud-dled that the true gospel is still a mystery to her. Can such a person, who so totally misunderstands the purpose and nature of Calvary, be saved, even though she has prayed the 'sinner's prayer'? From my understanding of the true gospel I would have to say probably not. And if a multitude of these kinds of Marys are now flooding into the local church what kind of church is being created?

The gospel of fulfilment

G. A. Pritchard, after spending a year studying the ministry at Willow Creek, eventually came to the conclusion that 'Bill Hybels believes that Harry's most important concern is for his personal fulfilment...Hybels teaches that Christianity will satisfy Harry's felt needs and provide fulfilment...Hybels and the other speakers do not condemn the search for fulfilment. Rather they argue that Harry has not searched in the right place. The question remains the same, but the answer has been changed. Harry asks, "How can I be happy?" "Accept Jesus", answers Hybels.'[19] Pritchard's analysis is correct,

> Is Willow Creek correct in their teaching that a relationship with Christ will provide a life of fulfillment? In a word, no... [But] personal fulfillment is the dominant goal of the vast majority of Americans. In this context it is a great temptation for American evangelicals to argue that Christianity is a means to fulfillment and the church becomes another place that promises to satisfy emotional desires...To argue for Christianity primarily by pointing to its usefulness in satisfying felt needs is to ultimately undercut it. To teach Christianity as a means eventually teaches that it is superfluous. If someone is able to satisfy his or her felt needs without Christ, the message of Christianity can be discarded...The bottom line why individuals should repent and worship God is because God deserves it. Fulfillment theology does not reflect the teaching of the Bible. We find in Scripture vast evidence that Christianity is often not 'fulfilling', Jesus promises his disciples that 'in this world you will have trouble.'...The Lord did not promise fulfillment, or even relief, in this world, but only in the next.... Fulfillment is not a spiritual birthright of Christians. The goal of a Christian's life is faithfulness, not fulfillment.[20]

Sociologist Robert Wuthnow, attempting to examine modern Christianity, 'suggests that in contemporary America, God has been moulded to satisfy people's needs...God is relevant to contemporary Americans mainly because the sense of God's presence is subjectively comforting; that is, religion solves personal problems rather than addressing broader questions.'[21] Bill Hybels, and his like-minded friends, knows from surveys and polls what unchurched Harry and Mary want in a God, and so presents a sanguine portrayal of God that could be summarized, 'God loves you and will meet you where you are, forgive you, and meet your felt needs and make you fulfilled.'[22] John MacArthur comments, 'Marketing savvy demands that the offense of the cross must be downplayed. Salesmanship requires that negative subjects like divine wrath be avoided. Consumer satisfaction means that the standard of righteousness cannot be raised too high. The seeds of a watered-down gospel are thus sown in the very philosophy that drives many ministries today.'[23]

Many within the new-paradigm church would loudly proclaim that salvation is by grace alone, through faith alone, in Christ alone. But they have redefined salvation. Salvation is not simply, under the new gospel, the forgiveness of sin and the imputation of righteousness. It is not a deliverance from the wrath of God upon a deserving and rebellious people.

The new gospel is a liberation from low self-esteem, a freedom from emptiness and loneliness, a means of fulfilment and excitement, a way to receive our heart's desires, a means of meeting our needs. The old gospel is about God; the new gospel is about us. The old gospel is about sin; the new gospel is about needs. The old gospel is about our need for righteousness; the new gospel is about our need for fulfilment. The old gospel is foolishness to those who are perishing; the new gospel is attractive. Many are flocking to the new gospel but it is altogether questionable how many are actually being saved. In a moment of reflection on the validity of the methods used at Willow Creek Hybels asked the Willow Creek congregation, 'How many of us have been vaccinated with a mild case of Christianity? How many among us have the real disease?'[24] This is the very question that concerns me after examining the 'New Gospel' being preached today.

John MacArthur is right when he states, 'Nothing in Scripture indicates the church should lure people to Christ by presenting Christianity as an attractive option...The message of the cross is foolishness to those who are perishing (1 Cor. 1:18). There is no way to make it otherwise and be faithful to the message...The gospel itself is disagreeable, unattractive, repulsive, and alarming to the world. It exposes sin, condemns pride, convicts the unbelieving heart, and shows human righteousness – even the best, most appealing aspects of human nature – to be worthless, defiled, filthy rags (cf. Isa. 64:6).'[25]

Spurgeon warned his day, 'when the old faith is gone, and enthusiasm for the gospel is extinct, it is no wonder that people seek something else in the way of delight. Lacking bread, they feed on ashes; rejecting the way of the Lord, they run greedily in the path of folly.'[26]

Peter Jennings, to my knowledge, is not a believer, but in the video *In the Name of God* he asks a thought provoking question: 'As these churches try to attract sell-out crowds are they in danger of selling out the gospel?' It is a worthy question. Wells's assessment is close to the truth, 'The church is losing its voice. It should be speaking powerfully to the brokenness of life in this postmodern world and applying the balm of truth to wounds that are fresh and open, but it is not. It is adrift.'[27]

A Church Focused On The Wrong Need

The new-paradigm church cannot be truly understood without an understanding of the influence of entertainment upon everything from its preaching to music. As documented in chapter two, entertainment has become a way of life and has permeated all aspects of society and culture. If, in fact, so much the American people say and do is defined by entertainment, then we are not surprised to find that entertainment has encroached upon the church as well. After all, even the best churches are comprised of redeemed sinners who have been shaped all too thoroughly by the world in which they live. And although the Bible clearly warns us not to be conformed to the world's image (Rom. 12:2), that battle unfortunately is not easily won. The reason being, at least in part, is that we often define nonconformity to the world in terms of externals — how we dress, what we eat or drink, where we go — while ignoring the philosophy of the world system that tends to creep into our hearts and minds. Many believers who would never think of taking a drink or dressing immodestly are nevertheless quite worldly in philosophy. They have taken a page out of society's playbook and developed corresponding lifestyles. In other words, they think like unbelievers. They approach the issues of life like unbelievers. They solve their problems like unbelievers. They make decisions like unbelievers, and usually they have no concept that this is how they live. Nowhere is this more apparent than in the area of amusement. If this is the case, it may be because few Christians have ever thought deeply on the subject of entertainment, and even fewer understand the danger.

Although entertainment has roots that go back many years, recently it has been developed into an art form. Something is behind this insatiable desire for amusement and fun. I believe that *something* is the relatively recent philosophy of self-fulfilment that has emerged out of the 1960s. 'Baby boomers have reoriented our society towards peers and away from family. They have moved the psychic center of the family away from obligations to others and toward self-fulfillment.'[1] The so-called need for personal fulfilment, I am convinced, is what propels this generation. Personal fulfilment is what people want, what they crave, what they will have. Entertainment is but one of the avenues travelled in search of fulfilment, or happiness.

It should not surprise us to discover that such a society has remade the church in its own image. 'A generation so at odds with the traditions it has inherited is going to change the way it does church…The generation that has crowded into maternity wards and grade schools and rock concerts now crowds into megachurches (only a generation that loved Woodstock could love Willow Creek). The generation that reorganized family around the ideal of self-fulfillment has done the same with religion. Surveys consistently show that baby boomers – whether evangelical or liberal, Protestant or Catholic – attend church not out of loyalty, duty, obligation, or gratitude, but only if it meets their needs.'[2]

Fulfilment

One of the ways in which this generation believes their need for fulfilment is met is through entertainment. The seeker-sensitive church has caught this wave all too well. They understand that this age is seeking fulfilment, and often in an entertaining format. They have designed their churches to meet this 'need', which largely explains their phenomenal growth, but it also is their greatest weakness. Os Guinness recognizes this when he writes, '[Take for example] the megachurches subordination of worship and discipleship to evangelism, and all three to entertainment, a problem that is already the Achilles heel of evangelicalism.'[3] It must be understood, at this point, that entertainment within the church comes in a variety of wrappings and the more subtle the wrapping the more dangerous the content. For example, when I am being entertained in either a secular or ecclesiastical setting, and know I am being entertained, it is of little consequence. If I go to a so-called Christian event which for the most part is light-hearted, full of laughter and fun music, I have gone to be entertained. I am not in attendance to worship God or be instructed in his Word. If I understand the purpose of my attendance is to have a good time, and as long as the entertainment is not out of sync with Christian character and biblical truth nothing is harmed. This boat springs a leak, however, the moment I begin to believe that this activity is worship or that this is the way worship should be packaged. As long as I can distinguish amusement from worship I can appreciate both in their proper setting. It is not wrong to be entertained as a Christian; it is wrong to confuse it with, or allow it to replace true worship and biblical instruction. 'The purpose of worship is clearly to express the greatness of God and not simply to find inward release or, still less, amusement.'[4]

Herein enters one of the subtlest forms of entertainment as related to the Christian and the church. The desire increasingly being uttered, by a self-fulfilment seeking generation, is the desire to experience or feel the presence of God (not to be confused with a genuine passion to know and worship a most holy God). Increasingly, Christians say they attend church to experience God, to come into his presence, to have a divine rendezvous. They want to go to a church where they can 'feel God'. George Gallup's assessment of the church based on his polls and surveys is, 'We are having a revival of feeling but not of knowledge of God. The church today is more guided by feelings than by conviction. We value enthusiasm more than informed commitment.'[5]

There are a number of pitfalls imminent in this desire; the most obvious of which is that it is unbiblical. Where in the Bible are we told to seek the presence of God as a felt experience? As New Testament believers we are already in the presence of God since he resides in our bodies (1 Cor. 6:19). And since Christ is our High

Priest we are told 'to draw near with confidence to the throne of grace' (Heb. 4:16). But nowhere in Scripture are we told to seek an experience in which we feel the presence of God. I often ask people who are caught up in this 'experiencing God' current, 'Exactly what does God's presence feel like?' After a fumbling attempt to explain, my next question is, 'How do you know that what you felt is God and not the devil, or your own imagination or last night's pizza?' They have no legitimate answer to this question, except 'they just know'. But that is not enough. If God did not see fit to demand us to seek such a divine experience, nor to describe what one would feel like, who are we to make this the apex of the Christian life of worship? Every Christian leader, especially in this age of quasi-mysticism, should read William James's old classic, *The Varieties of Christian Experience*, which, while not a Christian book, gives great insight into the claimed experiences emanating from all forms of religion. This volume should give us pause before so quickly pronouncing so many feelings and experiences as encounters with God. After a lifetime of studying religious people and their experiences, James offers this damning assessment, 'So long as men can use their God, they care very little who he is, or even whether he is at all...God is not known, he is not understood, he is used.'[6] Such an indictment should never be true of the child of God.

Still more germane to our subject is the reality that the 'feeling the presence of God' stampede is actually a form of entertainment with a thin layer of worship draped over it. This recent hunger for Divine encounter is precipitated by an appetite for personal fulfilment. A culture that so prizes personal fulfilment has found that one of the ways they can do this is through what they believe is experiencing God. Many are seeking the presence of God simply because it makes them feel better. 'Modern evangelicalism,' writes Donald Bloesch, 'has shamefully adapted to the therapeutic society, which makes personal fulfillment the be all and end all of human existence.'[7] This is entertainment (a focusing on our gratification and pleasure), not worship (focusing on the greatness of God), and it is a shameful form of entertainment because it tries to make God the servant to our desires ('using God' as William James called it).

That this is rapidly becoming the status quo in evangelicalism is evident by the number of Christians who now choose a church on the basis of musical styles and other superficial features, rather than on the ground of whether truth is being taught and God is being honoured. Growing churches, claims Christian A. Schwarz, are characterized by inspiring worship. In defining inspiring worship (as we saw earlier), he writes, 'People who attend inspiring worship services unanimously declare that the church service is — for some Christians this is almost a heretical word — "fun".'[8] Fun (i.e. entertainment) has become the criteria by which a large number of people are choosing the church they will attend. Many are all too happy to sacrifice doctrine for a good time. Many will endure outright heresies to enjoy a pleasant experience or to 'feel the presence of God', even if that presence is generated by mood-altering methods more akin to manipulation than worship. Indeed, it is altogether likely that some are willingly being manipulated because they enjoy 'Christianity Lite'. Michael Horton understands where the Christian herd is headed:

> Probably the single word that most viewers believe best describes the [Christian television] broadcasts is 'inspirational'. But what does it mean to be 'inspire'? It is a feeling of being moved religiously. What determines the genuineness of the feeling of inspiration? What separates inspiration from entertainment? Perhaps the dividing line can be described this way: Genuine inspiration is an emotional response to a genuine encounter with the living God. Inspiration, therefore, is not an end in itself or even something we should seek. It is rather a result of seeking and meeting God in His way. Inspiration is the result of something profoundly God-centered. Entertainment is profoundly man-centered. In entertainment a person looks for what pleases and excites himself or herself.
>
> Entertainment gratifies the viewer emotionally. Whether it pleases God may be quite a secondary matter. Error can inspire. It can make people feel good, though it displeases and angers God. The electronic church too often is in the entertainment, not inspiration, business. One is more likely to meet

and be moved by singers and personalities than by God. And to mask the quality of their programs with the ambiguous term inspiration is quite dishonest.

One of the great tragedies of our time is that so many local churches are choosing to try to copy the electronic church. Many local churches are seeking to be attractive by emulating some of the easy, individualistic, and interesting features of the electronic church. This strategy is self-defeating because usually the local church cannot match the professional production and slick graphics of television. But more important, the strategy dishonors God by failing to be what He wants the local church to be.[9]

The biblical picture is that the believer may in fact experience many wonderful emotions as a result of his or her relationship with God. But those emotions should result from and be based upon biblical truth, not man-created substitutes that are manufactured to elicit an emotional response.

8

A Church That Misunderstands Worship:
How Shall We Then Preach?

Many see this entertainment form of worship we have been discussing as a fad that will pass through our land and ultimately vanish over the horizon. If so, it will leave behind a scorched earth full of discouraged and bewildered believers, or quasi-believers, who will not know where to turn next. Nevertheless, it would appear that some are already flying the coop. Donald G. Bloesch reported this recently in a *Christianity Today* article outlining the early signs of a backlash to the seeker-sensitive services so popular today:

> Evangelical Protestantism is in trouble today as an increasing number of business and professional people are searching for a new church. The complaint I hear most often is that people can no longer sense the sacred either in the preaching or the liturgy...Worship has become performance rather than praise. The praise choruses that have preempted the great hymns of the church do not hide the fact our worship is essentially a spectacle that appeals to the senses rather than an act of obeisance to the mighty God who is both holiness and love. Contemporary worship is far more ego-centric than theocentric. The aim is less to give glory to God than to satisfy the longings of the human heart. Even when we sing God's

praises the focus is on fulfilling and satisfying the human desire for wholeness and serenity.[1]

The nature of worship

Much of the confusion in all of these matters comes because we do
not understand the nature of worship. John 4:23 tells us that we
are to worship God in spirit and truth. I agree with John MacArthur,
who writes concerning this verse, 'True worship involves the intel-
lect as much as the emotions. It underscores the truth that worship is to be focused on God, not on the worshiper.'[2] Our worship
should be centred on God as we praise him, through word, song
and prayer, and as we edify the saints through the teaching of the
Scriptures so that they are enabled to live lives honouring to him.
To so honour and worship God, all that we do must emerge from
truth.

The modern church does not take issue with worshiping God
in spirit – if anything this component has been elevated at the expense of its soul mate, truth. In our increasingly postmodern society truth is out and relativism is in. Unchurched Harry comes to
church with this mindset, having been saturated with it all week
long, and so it is no wonder that many believe that the way to
Harry's heart is not through the proclamation of truth. For, as we
have seen, Harry is a pragmatist. His question is, 'Does Christianity work?' not 'Is it true?' If we are to reach this generation we
must recognize Harry's worldview and present him with a relevant
message of pragmatism. If we do not, Harry will simply reject the
things of God and move on to other things that are more adept at
meeting his needs.

But is this how Jesus and the apostles approached their world?
Did they compromise with the prevailing worldview of their time or
did they challenge it? Without copious proof-texting I believe the
answers to these questions are obvious. Paul warned the Colossians, 'See to it that no one takes you captive through philosophy
and empty deception, according to the tradition of men, according
to the elementary principles of the world, rather than according to
Christ' (Col. 2:9). From the inception of Christianity it has been the

calling of God's people to expose the darkness of sinful thinking and reveal the truth of God's marvellous light of truth. Why should this generation be any different? 'Nothing in Scripture,' MacArthur reminds us, 'indicates the church should lure people to Christ by presenting Christianity as an attractive option.'[3]

Actually, truth is the very backbone of the Christian faith. Christianity is not just another option on the platter of pragmatism. It is not just another 'ism' that works for some people. If that were the case we would have nothing to say to those who claim that another religion or endeavour works for them. On the playing field of pragmatism we are in competition with everything from Hinduism to drugs to the Playboy philosophy. Where we have a clear and distinct advantage is in the realm of truth. We are offering truth in the form of Jesus Christ and his Word. As our society moves more into the dark corner of postmodernism and relativism, our message will increasingly stand out. Why would the seeker-sensitive experts want to abandon this clear advantage? Because they believe that if we do not we will be hopelessly out of step with our times.

To what tune is secular mankind dancing these days? While many are still waltzing to the melody of modernity, that optimistic faith in human reason and resources, the minor chord of postmodernity is becoming more common. It is far beyond the scope of this book to analyze the roots and effects of postmodernism on our culture, but Guinness sums it up well:

> Postmodernism is a movement and a mood as much as a clear set of ideas, so it often feels as if it is everywhere and nowhere. Doubtless, this means it is blamed for too much as well as too little. There are, of course, telltale fingerprints that postmodernism leaves on all it touches – the rejection of truth and objective standards of right and wrong, the leveling of authorities, the elevation of the autonomous self as the sole arbiter of life and reality, the equalizing of cultures, the promotion of image over character, the glorifying of power, the resort to victim-playing and identity politics, the licensing of victims' right to lie, and so on.[4]

When the church sees itself surrounded by unchurched Harrys and Marys who no longer believe in truth, objective values or morals, it is obligated to choose a strategy to reach them. Evangelical church leaders in the past have chosen to challenge the unbeliever with the very truth they had rejected. After all, unbelievers have always despised God's truth; they even hate the light, which is why they are lost in their sins and will remain so until they accept the gospel. Those who responded to the truth would in previous generations be further trained in biblical theology that would aid them toward maturity in Christ. But modern church leaders tell us that this bird will not fly anymore. If Harry insists on rejecting truth they will make him an offer he can't refuse — all of his heart's desires in the package of Jesus. Unfortunately, in the process, the gospel and the truth contained within, is diluted. One leader, who has been involved in the church growth movement, nevertheless warns,

The gospel is confrontational in its very nature. Any presentation of the gospel that does not present a challenge to the unbeliever to radically change his or her thinking and attitudes toward God and His saving work in Christ is not the same gospel preached in the pages of the New Testament! Today, people can be happy, healthy members of evangelical churches without ever having to face a God who is anything more than a 'buddy', a Saviour who is anything more than an example, and a Holy Spirit who is anything more than a power source. And that can happen without faith, repentance, indeed, without conversion.[5]

The sufficiency of Scripture

Perhaps no issue is of more importance, when we are considering the communication of truth, than the source of truth. The evangelical church has long held that the ultimate source for all truth concerning life and godliness is the Bible. Most conservative churches, whether of the market-driven variety or not, continue to have similar statements in their church constitutions and would pledge allegiance to the authority of Scripture. But in practice the Word of God is increasingly taking a back seat to the managerial and the therapeutic. This is undoubtedly the case because Christian leaders no longer have confidence in the sufficiency of Scripture.

The Word of God today is under attack, not just by its enemies, but also by those who claim to be its friend. Of course, this is nothing new; we can trace such attacks throughout the ages. What is new in evangelical circles is the outward appearance. Let's back up for a look at recent church history. In the 1920s and 30s differences between conservative and liberal churches came to a head in America. Out of that controversy came new denominations, fellowships, schools, missions, etc., that distinguished themselves from those who no longer believed in biblical Christianity. These organisations were founded by believers who desired to hold fast and 'contend earnestly for the faith' (Jude 3). One of the big problems at that time (as it is today), was developing a consensus concerning the essentials of the faith. That is, what doctrinal truths are beyond dialogue? What must all Christians who claim to be orthodox believe, and conversely what can be left to individual convictions? In other words, what are the non-negotiables of the faith? A series of volumes published originally in 1909, and known as *The Fundamentals for Today* were an attempt to answer these questions. Written by some of the finest conservative scholars and church leaders of the day, *The Fundamentals* addressed the doctrines of Christology and soteriology, but almost one third of the essays concerned the reliability of Scripture. Emerging from this is what became known as the Fundamentalist movement. A Fundamentalist was one who adhered to the fundamentals of the faith, primarily as described in *The Fundamentals*. One of those fundamentals was the belief in an infallible and inerrant Bible. As time moved on those who would later call themselves evangelicals split off from Fundamentalism. Evangelicals still held to the fundamentals of the faith, but believed there was more room to compromise and work with those who deny some of the essentials. Of course, today there are many sub-groupings under these headings, but that is not our subject. Our point is that by definition, all Fundamentalists and evangelicals supposedly adhere to the belief that the Bible is the very Word of God, without error in the original and correct in all that it affirms.

The terms *inerrant* and *infallible* originally affirmed by implication the authority and sufficiency of Scripture. This is no longer the case. Today we have many who loudly proclaim a belief in both inerrancy and infallibility but deny sufficiency. By the sufficiency of Scripture it is meant that the Bible is adequate to guide us into all truth pertaining to life and godliness. Based upon such passages as 2 Peter 1:3, 2 Timothy 3:15-4:2, and Psalm 19, sufficiency means that the Scriptures alone (through the power of the Holy Spirit) are capable of teaching us how to live life, how to mature in godliness, how to handle problems in a God-glorifying way and how to know truth. The Bible needs no help from the wisdom and experiences of men. To be sure, God has so created his universe, and us, in such a manner that mankind is capable of discovering and learning much that enhances life. The Bible does not address every issue that we might consider important. For example, is stem-cell research wrong? Should we take vitamins, work in factories, drive vehicles that pollute the atmosphere and on and on? But the Word is the only source that contains the words of life. Only the Bible tells us what God is like, how to have a right relationship with him and how to please him. Yet, the vast majority of both evangelicals and Fundamentalists believe the Scriptures are either inadequate or incomplete in communicating what the Christian needs to know when navigating the important issues of life. Thus they believe that something in addition to the Bible is necessary.

The sufficiency of Scripture has always been difficult for some Christians to accept. Colossians 2 describes a church during the New Testament era that felt it was necessary to add several things to the Scriptures in order to move on to maturity. The church at Colosse apparently had come under the influence of the early stages of Gnosticism which taught that certain Christians were privy to a mystical source of knowledge beyond the Scriptures. If one wanted to move on to maturity, according to the Gnostics, they had to tap into this extra-biblical knowledge through their esoteric methods. The Colossians, under this influence, were leaving behind their early instruction concerning the Christian life (2:1-7) and were being deluded into adding at least five things to God's Word: secular philosophy, legalism, asceticism, pragmatism, and mysticism. Using this passage as a springboard we could conclude that when anything outside of Scripture is championed as a means of knowing God's truth, biblical sufficiency has been denied. By this definition we find the conservative Christian landscape literally swamped with those who claim to believe in the authority of the Bible, yet in practice deny it by their extra-biblical sources of obtaining truth and guidance.

Before going any further, maybe we should ask the question, 'Is biblical sufficiency biblical? Does the Word claim to be sufficient?' In reply, we are reminded of 2 Peter 1:3, 'Seeing that His divine power has granted to us everything pertaining to life and godliness, through the true knowledge of Him.' How is life and godliness obtained? Through the true knowledge of Christ, found only in the Word. 2 Timothy 3:16-17 reminds us that the 'Scriptures are inspired by God and are profitable for teaching, reproof, correction, and training in righteousness.' Why? — So that we might be 'adequate, equipped for every good work'. We have to wonder, if the Scriptures are adequate to equip us for **every** good work, and if they are able to lead us to **everything** pertaining to life and godliness, what else is needed? Why search beyond the Scriptures for the things that God says the Scriptures alone supply?

In our support of the doctrine of biblical sufficiency we can do more than proof-text. The whole thrust of Scripture implies that the Word alone is sufficient to teach us how to live life and find guidance in a manner that honours God. As a matter of fact, the burden of proof that something beyond the Scriptures (visions, man's wisdom, tradition, etc.) is needed lies with those who doubt sufficiency. Note the view of God's Word as found in Psalm 19. We are told that it 'is perfect and will restore the soul. It is sure, making wise the simple. It is right, rejoicing the heart. It is pure, enlightening the eyes. It is clean, enduring forever. It is true and righteous altogether. It is more desirable than gold, it is sweeter than honey'. There is no hint here that the Word is inadequate to equip us for whatever life throws our way. As the Psalmist praises the Scriptures he implies that there is no need of help from any outside source to enable us to know and please God with our lives. This is the picture that we get throughout the entire Bible.

Preaching the Word

If pastors have lost confidence in the power, authority and sufficiency of the Scriptures it is no wonder that they have abandoned
in droves the systematic, expository preaching of the Word. I rare-
ly visit a church or attend a Bible conference anywhere in which
the Scriptures are truly expounded. Story-sermons, pop-psychology lectures, 'Dear Abby' style counsel, drama, musical produc-
tions, and interpretative dance are replacing true preaching. John
MacArthur said it well: 'If preaching is to play its God-designed
role in the church, it must be built upon the Word of God...Much
preaching today emphasizes psychology, social commentary, and
political rhetoric. Bible exposition takes a back seat to a misguided
craving for relevance...Lamentably, there is a discernable trend in
contemporary evangelicalism away from biblical preaching and a
drift toward an experience-centered, pragmatic, topical approach
in the pulpit.'[6]

I remember when I was training for ministry, hearing Warren
W. Wiersbe admonish us 'preacher boys' that as pastors we were
not to focus on 'entertaining the goats, we were to feed the sheep'.
I believe in most churches today that the sheep are starving to
death but do not know it because they are stuffed full of spiritual
goat feed.

So what should be the focus of preachers when they stand before God's sheep? If entertaining them is not the high water mark
of the message, what is? John Piper, in his excellent little book, *The
Supremacy of God in Preaching,* offers wise words that we would
do well to ponder. He writes,

> People are starving for the greatness of God. But most of
> them would not give this diagnosis of their troubled lives...The
> greatness and the glory of God are relevant. It does not mat-
> ter if surveys turn up a list of perceived needs that does not
> include the supreme greatness of the sovereign God of grace.
> That is the deepest need. Our people are starving for God.
> They need someone, at least once a week, to lift up his voice
> and magnify the supremacy of God...One of the implications
> this has for preaching is that preachers who take their cue

from the Bible and not from the world will always be wrestling with spiritual realities that many of their hearers do not even know exist or think essential…If God is not supreme in our preaching, where in this world will the people hear about the supremacy of God? If we do not spread a banquet of God's beauty on Sunday morning, will not our people seek in vain to satisfy their inconsolable longing with the cotton candy pleasures of pastimes and religious hype? If the fountain of living water does not flow from the mountain of God's sovereign grace on Sunday morning, will not the people hew for themselves cisterns on Monday, broken cisterns that can hold no water (Jer. 2:13)?[7]

This is the kind of preaching that God's church needs today. We dare not minimize the hunger in the hearts of his people by offering substitutes that cannot truly satisfy. 'The seasons come and go, the trends arrive and depart, the popular mood shifts and changes, but the preacher's task remains the same: to proclaim God's Word faithfully.'[8]

A Church That Misunderstands Worship:
How Shoud We Then Sing?

It was stated in the last chapter that our worship should be centred on God as we praise him through Word, song and prayer, and as we edify the saints through the teaching of the Scriptures so that they are enabled to live lives honouring to him. To so honour and worship God, all that we do must emerge from truth. Most would agree with that, at least in theory if not in practice, when it comes to preaching and teaching the Scriptures, for this is clearly taught in the Word (1 Tim. 4:13; 2 Tim. 2-4; Acts 2:42; Titus 1:9; Col. 1:25). Music, unfortunately, often gets an exemption. But do we have any more right to sing heresy than we do to preach heresy? Again, MacArthur is correct when he writes:

> Music by itself, apart from the truth contained in the lyrics, is not even a legitimate springboard for real worship. Similarly, a poignant story may be touching or stirring, but unless the message it conveys is set in the context of biblical truth, any emotions it may stir are of no use in prompting genuine worship. Aroused passions are not necessarily evidence that true worship is taking place. Genuine worship is a response to Divine truth. It is passionate because it arises out of our love for God.[1]

When the church gathers for worship what is its biblical mandate? Is it to amuse and entertain? Is it to cater to the cry for fulfilment? Or is it to honour God in spirit and in truth? The difference lies largely in the area of focus. Are we zeroed in on ourselves or on our God? Once it is established that God, not ourselves, must be central in our worship we then must examine what we do in worship. Here our practice must be in line with our biblical understanding of God and the church.

How shall we then sing?

In the previous chapter we touched on the importance of preaching. Preaching has fallen out of favour in our entertainment age as a means of communicating God's truth. Even when seeker-sensitive ministers preach, they don't call it that and try mightily to make it look as if they are not preaching. Pulpits are taboo, notes are hidden, expository preaching is abandoned for 'relevant' topical dissertations, references to church history are rare, and doctrine is considered too heavy.

But when it comes to the modern church attempting to connect with this generation, a generation born and raised in the era of entertainment, nothing is more prominent than music. So, we are not surprised to find that one of the great attractions for many toward this new way of 'doing church' is its music. Many are choosing the church they will attend largely on the basis of the type and excellence of the musical offerings. This being the case it is important that we discern what role music plays, or should play, in corporate worship. Far too often in modern worship music's place seems to be that of setting a mood. With the right music and talented musicians it is possible to create almost any mood. Do we want happy people? Tearful? Reflective? Excited? Motivated? Music in capable hands is able to create all these moods and many others. But is the setting of a mood or atmosphere the biblical purpose of Christian music?

One of the few passages of Scripture that delivers insight on the theme of music in the setting of the local church is Colossians 3:16, 'Let the word of Christ richly dwell within you, with all wisdom teaching and admonishing one another with psalms and hymns and spiritual songs, singing with thankfulness in your hearts to God' (see also the parallel verse Eph. 5:19). When many Christians come to church services today they want to be made to feel a certain way, but the central role of music in the New Testament church is to be a partner with the teaching of the Word of God. While music is a unique way to praise God in worship, the ultimate evaluation of that music in the Christian environment should be whether or not it has aided in the process of helping 'the Word of Christ to richly dwell within' us. Just as the authority and truth of Scripture should dominate our preaching and teaching, so should it dominate our singing.

Music as teaching

More specifically, the apostle Paul informs us that music serves the role of teaching and admonishing. Christian music is at its best when it instructs in sound doctrine. Many of the great hymns, and some contemporary songs, are steeped in theology that reinforces the truths found in the Word. Conversely, music has often been used within the church to teach and promote a wide range of heresies and aberrant doctrines. It is a well-known fact that the 4th-century heretic Arius used music to spread his belief that Jesus was a created being and not fully God. While the church councils, such as that of Nicaea, condemned Arianism, it continued to be popular among the masses for decades because Arius's teachings were placed to music and sung by undiscerning congregations.

Of course much Christian music, both ancient and modern, teaches very little in the way of biblical truth. Contemporary Christian music, in particular, is long on inspiration and short on instruction. Most of the popular choruses that are making the rounds today are simple lyrics of praise that, when at their best, pinpoint a single truth which is repeated in one form or another throughout the song. One such chorus continuously repeats the phrase, 'I exalt Thee, O Lord.' Well and good, he is worthy of exaltation. But why is he exalted? What enlightenment is given concerning the worthiness of God? Another chorus encourages us, based on Psalm 103, to 'Bless the Lord, O my soul...For He has done great things' (3 times). But if you read Psalm 103 the remaining 21 verses tells the reader why our souls should bless the Lord. Leonard Payton, in commenting on this particular chorus writes, 'What those great things are is left to the imagination, not the plain teaching of Scripture. The problem is that true, biblical gratitude must have its basis in objective facts or doctrine. If it doesn't, it is mere sentimentality.'[2] With this in mind, do the modern praise choruses have a place in our worship services? I personally believe that they do, but that place could be likened to the place of dessert in our diet. Almost everyone loves dessert, but dessert must not be the main feature of our daily diet or we will suffer grave consequences. To me, praise choruses are best used as a response to more substantial communications of truth, rather than the primary means of that communication. To make them the principle mainstay of a church's musical diet is to fatten the church on sweets when it needs a substantial helping of healthy food.

It might be of great value at this point to reflect upon the views of some of our respected church leaders from the past in relationship to music. Martin Luther said, 'Music is the handmaiden of theology.' His enemies, recognizing the truth of Luther's words lamented, 'Our people are singing their way into Luther's theology.'[3] *Christian History Magazine* reports that Charles Wesley's hymns included verses from every book in the Bible except Nahum and Philemon. He viewed his hymns as a primer in theology and a guide for public worship and private devotion.[4] Isaac Watts, the father of English hymnology, wrote hymns to complement his sermons.[5]

By contrast, much contemporary Christian music bypasses the mind and aims directly at the emotions. When the purpose of music is to elicit an emotional response devoid of biblical truth and with disregard to aiding in the process of 'the word of Christ dwelling in us richly', the net result is a romanticized Christian faith. Hearts can be moved by the skilful use of melodies and rhythm no matter what message a given song is conveying. For example, who has not felt a few goose bumps when an excellent performance of *The Battle Hymn of the Republic* has been given? But the lyrics of *The Battle Hymn of the Republic* were written by Julia Ward

Howe, a liberal Unitarian who believed in the fatherhood of God over all mankind. Her hymn has nothing to do with the spreading of the gospel, or the return of Christ, but rather with the eventual dominion of humanistic 'truth' over the entire world. It became a famous patriotic song but is hardly a hymn that teaches biblical truth.[6] We may enjoy the beauty and passion of the song but its theology is not helping the Word of Christ to dwell richly within us, and thus it is not a proper hymn for the church.

Many modern choruses teach questionable doctrine as well. Jack Hayford's *Majesty*, for example, teaches that 'kingdom authority flows from the throne unto His own'. This 'kingdom now' theology, which sees the church in the kingdom, or synonymous to it, is very prevalent among many charismatic and Latter Rain teachings. Armed with this understand of the church many such as Hayford, the Vineyard Movement, and the Word of Faith pundits believe that miracles, 'faith-healing', and other supernatural manifestations of the Spirit, should be common today. Those who reject such an understanding of the church age would be wise to note that they may be preaching one theology from the pulpit and singing another in the pew. If church leaders do not believe in the theology behind *Majesty* (and a host of other songs springing from the charismatic camp), they would be wise to eliminate these choruses from their musical agenda.

But what of the choruses and contemporary Christian songs that do teach biblical truth? While they surely may have a place in our worship, their weakness is that so often they offer praise to God but with a minimal doctrinal base. David Wells analyzed 406 songs contained in the *Worship Songs of the Vineyard Maranatha!* and *Music Praise Chorus Book*, along with 662 hymns of a traditional hymnal, *The Covenant Hymnal*, for their doctrinal content. Songs that simply mentioned a truth but did not elaborate on that truth were considered lacking in doctrinal content in his study. For example, a song that repeated throughout that Jesus is Lord, but nothing else, would not be counted among those with theological content. On the other hand, the relatively contemporary song *Meekness and Majesty* would be counted because of its development of his incarnation. This song does not simply say that Jesus is Lord but opens, 'Meekness and majesty, manhood and Deity, in perfect harmony, the Man who is God. Lord of eternity, dwells in humanity; kneels in humility and washes our feet.' This is an excellent example of utilizing music to teach solid theology.

Using the above criteria Wells claimed that 58.9 per cent of the praise songs he analyzed offer no doctrinal grounding or explanation for the praise. By contrast, among classical hymns 'it was hard to find hymns that were not predicated upon and did not develop some aspects of doctrine.'[7]

It would seem to me that if we are evaluating Christian music by how it aids in the process of 'the word of Christ dwelling in us richly', as opposed to how it makes us feel or its entertainment value, then that music should be steeped in scriptural truth. Additionally, if we analyze Christian music by comparing it with the Psalms, the biblical hymnbook, we would come to the same conclusion. The Psalms are not a collection of simple themes sung in repetitive fashion. They are, instead, absolutely full of doctrinal elaboration. They developed marvellous themes (in great detail). This is true of almost any Psalm but take Psalm 36 for example. Here the psalmist, David, contrasts the evil schemes of wicked men (vv. 1-4) with the loving-kindness of God (vv. 5-12):

> The words of his mouth are wickedness and deceit; He has ceased to be wise and to do good. He plans wickedness upon his bed; He sets himself on a path that is not good; He does not despise evil.

> Thy lovingkindness O Lord, extends to the heavens,
> Thy faithfulness reaches to the skies.
> Thy righteousness is like the mountains of God;
> Thy judgments are like a great deep.
> O Lord, thou preservest man and beast.
> How precious is thy lovingkindness, O God!
> And the children of men take refuge in the shadow of thy wings.
> They drink their fill of the abundance of thy house;
> And Thou dost give them to drink of the river of thy delights.
> For with thee is the fountain of life;
> In thy light we see light.

Today we might write, and sing, a song that simply repeats the truth of God's loving-kindness. Hugh Mitchell has written just such a chorus, which reads, 'Thy loving-kindness is better than life, Thy loving-kindness is better than life, my lips shall praise Thee, thus will I bless Thee, I will lift up my hands unto Thy name.' While there is nothing wrong in Mitchell's little chorus, and it is enjoyable to sing, the richness and depth of the psalm from which it is drawn are striking by contrast. The psalmist wrote of the manifold extent of not only God's loving-kindness but of his faithfulness, righteousness, and even judgments. He developed word pictures of the security, abundance, delights, life and light found in our Lord. Then he warns himself and his readers of the traps that are along life's highways that just might spring upon the unsuspecting child of God, 'Let not the foot of pride come upon me, and let not the hand of the wicked drive me away. There the doers of iniquity have fallen; they have been thrust down and cannot rise' (vv. 11-12). What a marvellous example the Psalms demonstrate for us with regard to proper use of music in our worship of God.

Music as admonition

Christian music is also to admonish, according to the New Testament. The Greek word for admonish means, 'to warn, to counsel, to correct'. A proper role of the church's music is to go beyond teaching to the application of that instruction. Music should point out danger, call us to attention, and advise us on how to make proper choices. Most Christian music, hymn or chorus, is sadly weak in this regard, but not so the Old Testament 'hymnal' — the book of Psalms. Psalms is loaded with this very type of admonishment. Take for example Psalm 95. Verses six and seven call us to worship a worthy God,

> Come, let us worship and bow down;
> Let us kneel before the Lord our Maker.
> For He is our God, and we are the people of His pasture,
> and the sheep of His hand.

This call to worship is immediately followed with warning and admonishment,

> Today, if you would hear His voice,
> Do not harden your hearts, as at Meribah,
> As in the day of Massah in the wilderness;
> When your fathers tested Me,
> They tried Me, though they had seen My work.
> For forty years I loathed that generation,
> And said they are a people who err in their heart,
> And they do not know My ways.
> Therefore I swore in My anger,
> Truly they shall not enter into My rest.

Perhaps a return to a steady diet of singing the Psalms (as is still practiced in some circles), or at least a careful examination of the employment of music in the Old Testament, would be a wise move for those interested in allowing music to fulfil its biblical purpose. That said, we would quickly add that the Psalms, as wonderful as they are, are nevertheless limited to Old Testament truth and so could not provide a balanced musical diet for the New Testament saint.

Speaking of the Psalms, it is time to note that Colossians 3:16 tells us that we are to 'teach and admonish one another with psalms, hymns, and spiritual songs'. I have heard this explained a number of ways but perhaps the most helpful was to learn that the Septuagint (the Greek translation of the Old Testament used often and quoted by Jesus and the apostles) labelled the 150 psalms alternatively as 'psalms', 'hymns' or 'spiritual songs'.[8] This is almost beyond question the backdrop of Paul's statement in Colossians. If so, a thorough study of how the Psalms teach and admonish might be the most profitable undertaking that Christian music leaders could do. At the very least the student will discover that the Psalms not only major on praising God but do so in the context of truth in a messy world. The Psalms deal with almost every conceivable circumstance in life but do so through the lens of God and his marvellous works. What could serve as a better guide for our ministry in music today?

'Whatever else Paul's admonition means, even a loose reading indicates that our worship music must regularly touch the entire superstructure of Christian doctrine.'[9] If this is true, and I believe it to be, then we must examine not only what our music says (and teaches) but also what it does **not** say. If songs played over Christian radio and in the market driven church are any indication, it would appear that the prominent theme in Christian music at the present time is that of God as 'felt need' meeter. If we are lonely, sad, hurting, disappointed or empty, come to Jesus who will comfort and fix what hurts. Depending on how it is presented there is truth in what these songs convey. Christ does comfort us and meet our true needs, especially that of righteousness. He calls us to the throne of grace to receive mercy and find grace to help in time of need (Heb. 4:16).

There is nothing wrong with singing of God's helping hand in times of pain and concern. But there is something wrong with doing so at the expense of other essential doctrines. God is more than a comforter. The Scriptures teach more than a handful of themes. The whole counsel of God needs to be explored, not only in our preaching but in our singing as well. Some of these themes will not play well with modern audiences, but they didn't play well with ancient ones either. When the author of Hebrews wanted to explain the Melchizedek priesthood of Christ to his readers he knew he had a problem; they had grown dull of hearing and could no longer digest solid theology (Hebrews 5:11-14). So what did he do? After a lengthy admonishment (5:11-6:20), he ploughed ahead anyway (chapters 7-10). His audience would have surely rather read a treatise on how God would make them feel better than about the life and significance of Melchizedek as a biblical type of Christ, but what they needed was an understanding of Melchizedek — and that is what he gave them. We would do well to pay attention to this pattern.

What should we do?

If we are serious about our Christian music being more than entertainment there are numerous things we could do, recognizing of course that we will probably be swimming up stream against the fads of the moment. After all, many Christians have listened to numerous hours of Christian radio, have attended Christian concerts, have been playing CDs recorded by professional Christian artists, and they are coming to church services expecting all of this to be duplicated on Sunday morning.

First, we should evaluate all the music we sing in our churches. Does it teach solid theology? Does it admonish us to correct living? Does it worship God in truth? Does it aid in the process of allowing the Word to dwell in us richly? The latter phrase means, by the way, that by study, meditation and application of the Word, it richly becomes at home in our lives. It has become a part of us. Does our music facilitate this process? Payton suggests we ask ourselves the following questions each Sunday, 'Did the music ministry today cause the word of Christ to dwell in us richly? Did we teach and admonish one another with gratitude in our hearts to God for Christ's finished work on the cross?'[10] This would be a worthy exercise.

Second, churches must receive training regarding this whole area of entertainment. Appetites can be developed. We must not cave in to the world's way of thinking. Entertainment has its place, but that place is not centre stage in the life and worship of Christ's church. The fact that the churches which have mastered the art of entertainment are growing by leaps and bounds should elicit extreme caution, not imitation, from those who understand the Scriptures.

Third, we could study with great profit the Psalms to discover how music is to be used to accomplish its biblically mandated goal.

Fourth, we need to teach our children good Christian music within the context of the church. They have the rest of their week to listen to whatever music they and/or their parents choose, but when they come to worship God corporately we must expose them to psalms, hymns, and spiritual songs, that will aid in the Word of Christ dwelling in them richly. They may not immediately like the tunes or the lyrics, but where else are they going to learn this great body of music if not in our churches?

A final consideration

Passion and emotionalism are often and easily confused in the modern church. The Christian life runs the full range of emotions: joy, peace, delight, love, sorrow, grief, concern, etc. Ours is a faith not only of the head but also of the heart. As a result it is right and proper to desire spiritual experience. The problem is that many Christians cannot tell the difference between enthusiasm for God and manipulation of the moment. Entertainment can look strangely like worship; fun can masquerade as joy; fleshly excitement can be perceived as divine encounter.

Part of our enigma today is that out of the free-love (i.e., drugs, sex) revolution of the 1960s has sprung an insatiable desire for experience. Experience has mounted the throne and barks out orders to a doting constituency that has lost patience in a world that does not make sense. If we cannot understand life, if in fact life makes no sense, at least we can enjoy ourselves. If it feels good it may not be right but it is better than nothing.

Unfortunately this attitude has crept into the church. Christians too want an experience that makes them feel good. So dominating has this desire become that truth is increasingly taking a back seat to a good time. Nowhere is this more evident than in our music.

The reaction of the concerned Christian is to be ever mindful that the Word, and not our experience, is our authority. True delight in God should emerge from biblical truth. Next, as has been mentioned above, we should take a good look at the Psalms to study the kind of music that pleases God and accomplishes his purposes. There we find the writers absolutely in love with and excited about their Lord. For example, Psalm 103:17-22 reads

> But the lovingkindness of the Lord is from everlasting to
> everlasting on those who fear Him,
> And His righteousness to children's children,
> To those who keep His covenant,
> And who remember His precepts to do them.
> The Lord has established His throne in the heavens;
> And His sovereignty rules over all.
> Bless the Lord, you His angels,

Mighty in strength, who perform His word,
Obeying the voice of His word!
Bless the Lord, all you His hosts,
You who serve Him, doing His will.
Bless the Lord, all you works of His,
In all places of His dominion;
Bless the Lord, O my soul!

Here is a man (David) finding great joy in his Lord. He is not wrapped up in the side issues; he is not drumming up feelings; he is not being whipped into a mood. He is simply reflecting on his God and his heart can hardly contain what it views. This is the spiritual experience we should crave.

10

The Gospel According to Warren

No one has exemplified the market-driven approach better than Rick Warren, pastor of the huge Saddleback Church in southern California and author of *The Purpose-Driven Church* and *The Purpose-Driven Life*. While Warren is open and up-front about his philosophy, strategy and methods, nevertheless things are not always as they appear. For example, 'purpose-driven' sounds better than 'market-driven' but it is basically the same thing. In his book *The Purpose-Driven Life*, his opening statement is, 'It is not about you'; Warren then writes a whole book about 'you'. He belittles pop-psychology but repeatedly promotes it throughout the book. He publicly cuts ties with Robert Schuller, but reiterates some of the most odious things Schuller has been teaching for thirty years. He claims commitment to the Scriptures but undermines them at almost every turn. He will tell his followers that he is not tampering with the message but only reengineering the methods, when in fact he has so altered the message that it is no longer recognisable.

This brings us to his most disturbing alteration, the gospel itself. To charge Warren with modifying the gospel is a serious accusation, one that should not be made lightly. What is the evidence for such an indictment? Consider the following:

In the video that accompanies the '40 Days of Purpose', Warren leads his listeners in prayer at the end of the first session. The prayer goes like this:

> Dear God, I want to know your purpose for my life. I don't want to base the rest of my life on wrong things. I want to take the first step in preparing for eternity by getting to know you. Jesus Christ, I don't understand how but as much as I know how I want to open up my life to you. Make yourself real to me. And use this series in my life to help me know what you made me for.

Warren goes on to say:

> Now if you've just prayed that prayer for the very first time I want to congratulate you. You've just become a part of the family of God.

Warren would be hard-pressed to find biblical backing for this presentation of the gospel. We find nothing here about sin, grace, repentance, the Person of Christ, Calvary, faith, judgement, or the resurrection. This is the ultimate in a mutilated, seeker-sensitive gospel: the seeker comes to Christ in order to find his purpose in life, not to receive forgiveness from sin and the righteousness of God. Then, to pronounce someone a full-fledged member of the family of God because he has prayed such a prayer (based on minimal, if any, understanding of the person and work of Christ), is beyond tragic.

Does Warren do any better in his book, *The Purpose-Driven Life?* — a little, but not much. Concerning eternity he tells his readers, 'If you learn to love and trust God's Son, Jesus, you will be invited to spend the rest of eternity with him. On the other hand, if you reject his life, forgiveness, and salvation, you will spend eternity apart forever' (p. 37). There is just enough truth here to be confusing, but the New Testament never tells us to learn to love and trust Christ in order to be saved. We are told to repent (Acts 17:30) and place our faith in Christ (Eph. 2:8-9), not 'learn to love and trust'. Just how does the unbeliever go about learning to love and trust Jesus? These are fruits of regeneration, not means to regeneration.

On page 58, Warren gives perhaps his most complete gospel presentation found in *The Purpose-Driven Life*. There he tells his readers that they must first believe God loves them and has chosen them to have a relationship with his Son who died on the cross for them. Warren writes, 'Real life begins by committing yourself completely to Jesus Christ.' I would not argue with that, but how are we to commit ourselves to Christ? Warren states, 'Right now, God is inviting you to live for his glory by fulfilling the purposes he made you for ...all you need to do is receive and believe.... Will you accept God's offer?' Again, he offers a sample prayer, 'I invite you to bow your head and quietly whisper the prayer that will change your eternity, "Jesus, I believe in you and I receive you."' He promises, 'If you sincerely meant that prayer, congratulations! Welcome to the family of God! You are now ready to discover and start living God's purpose for your life.' It is worth noting that this gospel presentation is found on Day 7 (of the 40-day journey). We are to assume that the content of Days 1-6 have led up to this invitation to receive Christ. What Warren believes a sinner needs to know to become part of the family of God has presumably been presented in the first week of the journey. But Warren has said nothing about who Jesus is, why he died on the cross, in what manner he is their Saviour, the cleansing power of the blood of Christ, repentance or confession of sin, the consequences of sin, or again, the resurrection of Christ.

In a biblically illiterate, post-Christian era, it cannot be assumed that the unbeliever has any concept of any of these things. This is especially disturbing in light of Warren's central message: find God and you will find yourself (purpose). When this is undeniably the thesis of *The Purpose-Driven Life*, and the 'Forty Days of Purpose' campaign, the unbeliever would naturally conclude that he is praying a prayer that will enable him to solve the problem of lack of purpose in his life. Where in the Scriptures is the gospel ever presented as Warren presents it? We are hopeful that Warren does not personally deny any of the essential elements of the gospel, but he certainly does not give them proper weight and he leaves much to the imagination of his readers.

John MacArthur writes, 'Listening to a seeker-sensitive evangelical preacher today, we're likely to think it's easy to be a Christian. Just say these little words, pray this little prayer, and poof! you're in the club.'[1] Admittedly, salvation is received by faith alone in Christ alone, but it is not received by mouthing a little prayer lacking in biblical content and understanding, with the hopes that you will find purpose in life. As a matter of fact, one evangelical leader is reported to have entitled a sermon in response to the seeker-sensitive gospel, 'How to Fill Your Church with Tares'.

MacArthur warns, 'People are breezing through those wide, comfortable, inviting gates with all their baggage, their self-needs, their self-esteem, and their desire for fulfillment and self-satisfaction. And the most horrible thing about it is they think they're going to heaven.'[2]

Ladies Home Journal

Warren's popularity with the masses has risen to such levels that he has now been asked to write a monthly column for the *Ladies Home Journal*. While some may question why a secular magazine would be interested in what an evangelical pastor has to say, certainly we can rejoice that Warren has been handed a worldwide forum (readership estimated at 14.5 million) in which to proclaim God's truth, including the gospel, to a largely unbelieving audience. What a privilege. He has been given a platform from which he can herald the excellencies of Christ. But, unfortunately, Warren has not done that. Rather than preach Christ, Warren's message, as reflected in the title of his article is, 'Learn to Love Yourself'. In his March 2005 article, the man who opened his book with the words, 'It's not about you', shows that he really thinks it is. He tells his readership, 'To truly love yourself, you need to know the five truths that form the basis of a healthy self-image.' What are they? (All the following are direct quotes from Warren's article):

Accept Yourself
God accepts us unconditionally, and in his view we are all precious and priceless. Focus on this and you will not waste any

time and effort trying to be someone you're not.

Love Yourself
[Warren's wife affirms], God really does love me without strings attached. [On this basis we apparently have been given the freedom to love ourselves]

Be True To Yourself
Discover, accept and enjoy our unique 'shape' [which refers to Warren's S.H.A.P.E. program]...Be content with them [our weaknesses].

Forgive Yourself
God doesn't expect perfection but He does insist on honesty. When I honestly admit my errors and ask forgiveness in faith, He doesn't hold a grudge, doesn't get even, and doesn't bring it up again. We should practice such a forgiving attitude with ourselves.

Believe in Yourself
Start affirming the truth about yourself! The truth is God has created you with talents, abilities, personality and background in a combination that is uniquely you. It's your choice. You can believe what others say about you, or you can believe in yourself as God does, who says you are truly acceptable, lovable, valuable and capable.

What a disappointment! Not only does Warren not share the gospel, the glory of Christ or any theological truth, he muddies the waters by offering anemic pop-psychology, none of which is supportable from Scripture. Briefly, remember that Warren is not writing to believers but to the general populace, which he would have to assume is largely unsaved. With that in mind consider:

First, to this audience he tells them that God accepts them unconditionally. Nothing could be further from the truth. We are unacceptable to God in our natural state. It would take the death of the Son of God to provide the means whereby we could be accepted by God and only those who are in Christ are acceptable to the Father (Ephesians 1:3-14).

Second, nowhere in Scripture are we ever told to love ourselves. We are told to love God with all of our heart, soul and mind. We are also told to love others as we love ourselves (Matt. 22:37-40). Some jump on this phrase, 'as yourself', as proof that God commands us to love ourselves. That is not true. The Scriptures tell us we already love ourselves (Eph. 5:28-29); we do not need to be encouraged to an inordinate self-love that amounts to self-centredness. As a matter of fact, the only passage in the New Testament that actually speaks of self-love considers it a sinful sign of the last days (2 Tim. 3:2). Christ calls us to deny self (Luke 9:23) not love self.

Third, to tell the unbeliever to accept and be true to himself is to condemn him eternally. Should one who is dead in his trespasses and sins (Eph. 2:1) be told to be content with his weaknesses? Warren may be attempting to soothe the troubled hearts of his readers, but he is not pointing them to the Saviour.

Fourth, not a word can be found in Scripture about forgiving ourselves. This is a modern psychological invention, not a biblical principle. God calls us to confess our sins to him and he will forgive us (1 John 1:9). We lack the ability and authority to forgive ourselves; that is God's prerogative.

Fifth, rather than believe in self we are told to 'believe on the Lord Jesus' (Acts 16:31). Rather than believe in self, Paul confirmed that we are inadequate in ourselves (2 Cor. 3:5), being mere earthen vessels (2 Cor. 4:7). Rather than believe in self we are told that anything we accomplish is through God's strength (Phil. 4:13). Rather than believe in self, Paul said that he 'boasted in his weaknesses, that the power of God may dwell in me' (2 Cor. 12:9).

How can this evangelical pastor, who has emerged as the most recognised Protestant leader in the world, one who is looked to for spiritual insight and guidance by millions, miss the mark so widely?

Perhaps the key is in his view of doctrine. In *The Purpose Driven Life,* Warren wants us to have no doubt that when we stand before the Lord 'God won't ask about your religious background or doctrinal views. The only thing that will matter is, did you accept what Jesus did for you and did you learn to love and trust him' (p. 34)? On the contrary, what we believe is of utmost importance. Did the Holy Spirit inspire the Bible for us to ignore what it teaches? Are the words of Jesus insignificant? Are the doctrinal truths of the New Testament epistles nothing more than filler? Concerning salvation, it does matter what you believe about Jesus, the cross, the resurrection, sin, judgement, the gospel and so forth. Warren is doing a great disservice to the church of God. As he minimizes the content of the gospel, trivializes Scripture, belittles doctrine and replaces them with psychology, mysticism and worldly wisdom, we are reminded of Paul's warning in Colossians 2:8, 'See to it that no one takes you captive through philosophy and empty deception, according to the tradition of men, according to the elementary principles of the world, rather than according to Christ.'

An alternative to Warren's methods and message

My wife and I recently attended a worship service of an evangelical church which has adopted the purpose-driven model popularized by Warren. The service was disturbing on a number of fronts, including irreverent worship, unbiblical musical selections and a general attitude of apathy. But what was most troubling was the sermon. The pastor, surely a well-meaning and sincere servant of God, had no clue how to exegete the Scriptures. In his topical message he pointed the congregation, by means of PowerPoint slides, to dozens of passages. But in astounding fashion he managed to misinterpret, either through spiritualizing, missing the context, reading a poor translation, etc., every single passage. Not once did he provide the correct interpretation of any verse of Scripture, yet as far as I could observe no one seemed to notice or care.

This gave me further insight into what I have been suspecting and observing. Warren's philosophy of ministry, misuse of Scripture, weak gospel message, infiltration of psychology and disregard for theology is being embraced by evangelicalism because that is where much of evangelicalism is already residing. Warren is not so much an initiator as he is a product of his time. I believe he has caught the wave of what was already happening in evangelicalism. What he has done successfully is connect the dots – develop methods, programs and a message that seems to work. Pragmatism has become the final arbitrator in our society and increasingly in our churches. 'If it works it must be of God', so goes conventional wisdom. But pragmatism is an unreliable trailblazer. In our more reflective moments few of us are willing to believe that success can always have the final word. For example, Mormonism is the most successful 'church' in the world today. Yet, none of us is willing to believe that God is blessing the Mormon Church. If pragmatism is our guide, we will be hopelessly tossed about by every wind of doctrine (Eph. 4:14). We need something more stable – a true foundation.

Back to the Bible

1 Timothy 3:15 describes the mission of the church as being the pillar and support of the truth. Whatever else the church does, it must take this commission from God seriously. No one but God's church is interested in such a project – it falls on God's people, the true church, to be the one place where truth is believed, upheld, and gloriously proclaimed. Of course, the truth that the church has to offer has a source – the Word of God. All the church does must emerge from the Scriptures. Every method, program, evangelistic effort, and message the church declares must find its roots firmly planted in biblical truth.

This leads us to Warren's and his imitators' Achilles' heal: Warren does not begin with the Bible. At first glance, 'The Purpose-driven' programs and message are quite attractive. They seem to speak the language of the people; they are successful; they are saturated with Scripture, much of its teaching is on the mark. Further, many who promote *The Purpose-driven Life* are sincere and well-meaning. But upon closer examination there is a fly in the soup. It is no ordinary fly either – it is a huge monstrosity, filled with deadly poison. We can attempt to ignore the fly, hoping all will be well, but ultimately we must either deal with the fly or allow it to alter our soup to something altogether different.

What is the fly? It is this – Warren does not begin with Scripture, he begins with people. His church was started on the basis of a survey asking people what they wanted in a church. He quizzes the congregation on the kind of secular music they like and provides that kind of music. He starts with the felt-needs of people and then crafts a message to meet those needs. He determines what he believes people want to hear and then goes to Scripture to find support for his philosophy of ministry.

It is right here that we need to step back and carefully examine the purpose-driven philosophy. I have found if you skip the foundation underlying any system that the superstructure can appear beautiful – for a time. Again take Mormonism. Its outward emphasis on family values and morals is certainly winsome. It is its foundation which is faulty. By the same token we need to examine *The Purpose-driven Life's* foundation. Has it been laid after careful study of the Scriptures? Or are its building blocks made of secular fads, philosophies and pragmatism, mortared together with careless use of Scripture? If the latter is your conclusion, as it is mine, what are we to do?

Believe it or not, there is an alternative to PDL and other such programs. It sounds simplistic and old fashioned but it has God's stamp of approval. It is a return to the Bible. Our pulpits need to return to the unabashed exposition of Scripture. Our Sunday school classes and Bible studies need to toss the manuals and guides written about the Bible and open the Bible itself. In our local church we have dropped all commercial Sunday school curriculum -- which has been watered down to the point of uselessness – and simply teach the Bible. Our 4-5 years old are being taught selected Bible stories. Ages 6-7 will go through the Bible from Genesis to Revelation in those 2 years. Ages 8-9 will go through the Bible yet again. Ages 10-11 are being taught hermeneutics and Bible study methods and applying those methods to the study of the epistles. Ages 12-13 are taught Bible-college-level courses on systematic theology. High school students are taught the Bible with emphasis on biblical discernment. At this level many of them begin to teach children as well as their peers. All adult courses are focused on the study of Scripture, along with classes on church history, theology, and biblical living. All sermons are verse-by-verse expositions of the Word. Certainly our teachers use commentaries and Bible study aids but it is the Scriptures themselves that are studied.

I have found an amazing thing – when people are fed a steady diet of biblical truth they have little craving for cotton-candy fads. Why would anyone trade in the fountain of life for cisterns that can hold no water (Jer. 2:13)? Of course many have and do, but the solution is not to crawl into the cistern, it is to showcase the fountain.

But this 'return to the Bible' approach has one fatal problem – we are in the midst of a crisis of confidence in the sufficiency and authority of Scripture. If we do not believe that God's Word is sufficient, then we will not showcase it. If we do not believe in the final authority of the Word then we will look for alternatives. What the church and the world need today are men and women of God who believe with all of their hearts in the sufficiency of his Word. We need a church that is not ashamed of Christ and his Word (Luke 9:26), a church that will boldly proclaim the truth from the housetops. It is reported that Charles Spurgeon once said, 'There is no need for you to defend a lion when he's being attacked. All you need to do is open the gate and let him out.' With Spurgeon, I believe it is time to once again open the gate and let the Word do its work.

11

A Church At The Crossroad

In the early days of the twentieth century the American church was embroiled in a great controversy that would ultimately result in a schism that exists to this day. The growing liberal wing of Christianity, having fallen in love with German higher criticism of the previous century, was challenging all that believers had held dear since the Reformation. Under attack, among other things, was the deity of Christ, the miracles, the inspiration of Scripture and the gospel itself. Rising to the challenge were men who called themselves Fundamentalists because they adhered to the fundamentals of the faith that they believed defined true Christianity. One of those early Fundamentalists was Princeton professor and Reformed theologian Benjamin B. Warfield. Warfield warned his generation of the consequences of compromising doctrine in order to accommodate and draw the unbeliever.

The moment a church [takes] up such a position, however, it would cease to be a Christian Church: the core of Christianity is its provision for salvation from sin. No doubt by the adoption of such a platform many would be recovered to the Church who now stand aloof from it. But this would be not because the world had been brought into the Church, but because the Church had been merged into the world. The offense of Christianity has always been the cross; as of old, so still today, Christ crucified is to Jews a stumbling-block and to Greeks foolishness. It would be easy to remove the offense by abolishing the cross. But that would be to abolish Christianity.[1]

The battle cry of the liberal church of Warfield's day was relevancy, just as today. The only way Christians, many believed, were going to impress and impact the world of their day was to incorporate secular philosophies and fads into the life of the church. The world had to see that the church was 'cool'; it was up-to-date; it was in keeping with the times. Again Warfield, offered wise words,

A theology which is to be kept in harmony with a growing science and philosophy and scholarship, breaking their way onward by a process of trial and correction, must be a veritable nose of wax which can be twisted in any direction as it may serve our temporary purpose. If it be asked, therefore, in what way 'the fundamental theology of the Church' 'is to be related to the literary, scientific, and philosophical certainties of our times,' the answer certainly cannot be that it is to be subordinated to them and made their slave, tremblingly following their every variation as they zigzag their devious way onward toward the certainties, not 'of our time,' but of all time.[2]

Warfield, and other like-minded defenders of the faith, were ignored by the major denominations resulting in the secularization of the church rather than the evangelizing of the world. Many people who recognized that these denominational churches had sold out, left, as we mentioned earlier, to form their own evangelical and Fundamental denominations, fellowships, schools and parachurch organisations. It is the descendents of these modern day reformers who are caving in to the same kind of forces that their fathers fought so bravely against.

History tells us that it would not be many years after the liberals of early 1900s 'won' their war against the Fundamentalists that their churches went into a decline from which they have not yet recovered. It did not take people long to realize that if the church was not offering anything significantly different from what the world offered then apparently the church was unnecessary. The liberal church marginalized itself through compromise with modernism. It ceased to be a light and became a reflection of the secular philosophies of the times.

The new-paradigm church of today is following the same pattern. Flushed with success she is rushing headlong down the slope of secularism. It will only be a matter of time before it is realized that this modern church having lost its message, having compromised the faith, having mistaken numerical success for the blessing of God, will implode, for there will be nothing left to sustain it. The fallout will undoubtedly harm many but hopefully God will raise a stronger church, a church serious about truth, a church that is more concerned about feeding the sheep than entertaining the goats, a church that knows the difference between worship and amusement, a church willing to be despised by the world for the sake of the cross — a church not ashamed of the true gospel, for it will know that the gospel is the power of God for salvation to everyone who believes.

Appendix
Repentance

If there is one element of the gospel message that is minimized today it is the doctrine of repentance. Some have eliminated it altogether; others have distorted and softened its meaning. Some have done so on theological grounds, others for more pragmatic reasons. On the pragmatic level we have to admit that repentance does not play out very well in a self-oriented, narcissistic society. Many are quite content to receive Christ if they can possess eternal life with no fundamental interference in their ungodly lifestyles. If repentance is thrown into the mix, it changes everything. If the gospel message is that Jesus Christ died for our sins, our response to the gospel is to believe and to place our faith in him for the forgiveness of sins. But is it possible to trust our Lord for forgiveness and the corresponding righteousness of God (2 Cor. 5:21) and at the same time continue to embrace our sins and idols? In other words, can we turn to Christ for forgiveness and have no intention of turning from sin? Paul did not think so (Acts 26:18,19). The biblical word for turning from sin is 'repentance', which, as I will attempt to demonstrate, is essential to one's experience of salvation. Repentance is not an additional step to faith; they represent two sides of the same coin.

The understanding that salvation is the result of God's *grace alone*, received through *faith alone* in *Christ alone*, was the cornerstone of the Reformation and is universally recognized by all true Fundamental/evangelical Christians. Nevertheless, all aspects of this trifold pronouncement of *alones* are under attack today within evangelical circles. For example, the gospel is the good news that God provides the gift of forgiveness, redemption and reconciliation, by grace alone. Yet, while all Christian branches would champion the idea of grace, it is becoming increasingly popular to understand that grace can be dispensed through certain sacraments or obtained as a result of certain efforts on our part. Correspondingly few would deny that salvation is based on Christ and his shed blood, but some are contending that even those who have never heard of Christ or his cross can find redemption. Fortunately, even as these heresies are gaining in popularity they are still hanging out on the fringes of the conservative church. As of yet they have not penetrated deeply into the heart of Bible-believing Christianity.

Of a more divisive nature is the recent battle over the second of the 'solas'. Again, all true evangelicals are in agreement that God's grace is received through the faith without works of any kind. The debate is over the *nature* of saving faith. Just exactly what is faith? In the past, from the Reformation through the mid-twentieth century, there was little question among conservative believers that saving faith included a turning *from* sin and a turning *to* God. Some representative quotes from a wide range of theological perspectives might help to demonstrate this fact. I do not endorse the theology of every individual mentioned below: they merely serve to show the wide-range of agreement on the subject from important Christian leaders in the recent past:

Charles Spurgeon (Reformed Baptist)

'Christ Jesus did not come in order that you might continue in sin and escape the penalty of it; he did not come to prevent the disease being mortal, but to take the disease itself away. . . . Christ did not come to save thee in thy sins but to save thee from thy sins.'[1]

William Booth (Methodist)

'The chief danger of the twentieth century will be: Religion without the Holy Spirit, Christianity without Christ, forgiveness without repentance, salvation without regeneration, and Heaven without Hell.'[2]

A. W. Tozer (Evangelical - Christian Missionary Alliance)

'Quasi Christians follow a quasi Christ. They want His help but not His interference. They will flatter Him but never obey Him'[3]

'It is altogether doubtful whether any man can be saved who comes to Christ for His help but with no intention to obey Him.'[4]

Benjamin Warfield (Reformed)

'We cannot be said to believe that which we distrust too much to commit ourselves to it.'[5]

J. I. Packer (Anglican)

'The repentance that Christ requires of His people consists in a settled refusal to set any limits to the claims which He may make on their lives. . . . He had no interest in gathering vast crowds of professing adherents who would melt away as soon as they found out what following Him actually demanded of them.'[6]

More recently, however, some have risen to challenge this understanding of our great salvation. The Westminster Shorter Catechism of 1647 (which represented the theological understanding of conservative Christians of that era and is still representative of many today) declared, 'Repentance unto life is a saving grace, whereby a sinner, out of a true sense of his sins, and apprehension of the mercy of God in Christ, doth, with grief and hatred of his sin, turn from it unto God.' And, 'Repentance unto life doth chiefly consist of two things — In turning from sin, and forsaking it.'[7]

Some, such as Charles Ryrie, on the other hand, have declared that repentance is nothing more than a change of mind about Christ and has nothing whatsoever to do with changing our minds about sin.[8] Others, like Zane Hodges, go further and say that preaching repentance to an unbeliever is adding works to the gospel.[9] While both men would agree that salvation is salvation not only to righteousness and eternal life, but also salvation (deliverance, rescue) from sin, neither believes that when the unbeliever turns to God he must also turn from sin. Therefore, according to these men an individual can turn to Christ, trust him for salvation, and ask for forgiveness, yet have absolutely no desire or intention to turn from sin and still be saved from sin and declared righteous.

Something is seriously wrong here. Is turning from sin as we turn to God part of the gospel message or is it not? As we have seen, fine, godly men are lined up on both sides of the issue. But the pronouncements of men, while serving as a reference point, are not our final source of truth. For that we must turn to the Scriptures.

Conversion

There are three Greek words, **epistrepho**, **metamelomai**, and **metanoeo**, found in the New Testament that deal with the concept of turning from sin and turning to God. The first of these words is **epistrepho** often translated 'to turn, return or be converted'. About half of its uses involve physical or secular turning. For example, the demon exorcised from a man says, *I will return (**epistrepho**) into my house from whence I came out* (Matt. 12:44). The rest of the uses of **epistrepho** have theological or spiritual implication — it is these we wish to examine.

'The basic meaning of **epistrepho** is turning around either in the physical or the mental or the spiritual sense of the term; and that thus when the word moves in the world of thought and religion it means a change of outlook and a new direction given to life and to action.'[10] A turn of any kind involves two things: a turning *from* something and a turning *toward* something. In the sphere of salvation conversion (**epistrepho**) means, on the one hand, a turning towards God. 'All who lived at Lydda and Sharon saw him, and they turned (**epistrepho**) to the Lord' (Acts 9:35). 'And the hand of the Lord was with them, and a large number who believed turned (**epistrepho**) to the Lord' (Acts 11:21). 'Therefore it is my judgment that we do not trouble those who are turning (**epistrepho**) to God from among the Gentiles' (Acts 15:19). 'For you were continually straying like sheep, but now you have returned (**epistrepho**) to the Shepherd and Guardian of your souls' (1 Pet. 2:25). Even in the Gospel of John, where we often find the concept of repentance, if not the word, we run into **epistrepho**. 'He has blinded their eyes, and hardened their heart, lest they see with their eyes, and perceive with their heart, and be converted (*epistrepho*), and I heal them' (John 12:40). To my knowledge very few would have a problem with the concept that saving faith involves a turning to God.

On the other hand a person cannot turn **to** someone or something without turning **from** something else. It is at this point that much controversy erupts. As a person turns to God for saving grace what is it that he turns from? An examination of the pertinent Scriptures clearly reveals that as one turns to God he simultaneously turns from sin. Let's look at the Scriptures: In 1 Thessalonians 1:9 Paul writes, 'For they themselves report about us what kind of a reception we had with you, and how you turned (*epistrepho*) to God from idols to serve a living and true God.' In turning to God the Thessalonians turned from their idols. Can one turn to God and yet continue to grasp their idols? Paul didn't think so. Turning to God and turning from idols was a packaged deal — inseparably linked.

When Paul was preaching the gospel at Iconium he was clear, 'Men, why are you doing these things? We are also men of the same nature as you, and preach the gospel to you in order that you should turn (*epistrepho*) from these vain things to the living God' (Acts 14:15). It is obvious that Paul did not envision someone turning to God without turning from 'vain things'. And remember, this was in the context of preaching the gospel, not instructions dealing with sanctification.

At Paul's conversion he was commissioned to the Gentiles in order 'to open their eyes so that they may turn (*epistrepho*) from darkness to light and from the dominion of Satan to God, in order that they may receive forgiveness of sin and an inheritance among those who have been sanctified by faith in Me' (Acts 26:18). The gospel preached, through the power of the Holy Spirit, would enable people to see truth in order that they might turn *from* something *to* something. They would turn from darkness (sin, evil) to light (righteousness), from the dominion or mastery of Satan to the dominion or mastery of God. And just so we don't misunderstand Paul's commission, note how he applied it to his own ministry: He went to the Gentiles preaching, 'That they should repent (*metanoeo* — see below for the meaning of this word) and turn (*epistrepho*) to God, performing deeds appropriate to repentance (metanoeo)' (Acts 26:20). Paul was not hesitant to call for repentance and conversion. He saw no incongruence between faith and repentance from sin. They were not separate steps, they were part and parcel of the same thing — the gospel.

The Dictionary of New Testament Theology (a standard and valuable source for word study) has this to say, 'When men are called in the NT to conversion, it means a fundamentally new turning of the human will to God, a return home from blindness and error to the Saviour of all (Acts 26:18; 1 Peter 2:25)...Conversion involves a change of Lords. The one who until then has been under the lordship of Satan (Ephesians 2:1-2) comes under the Lordship of God, and surrender of the life to God is done in faith, and includes the whole of life (Acts 26:20).'[11]

Regret

The next Greek word that we should consider is **metamelomai**, a word that is often confused with true repentance. It does carry the idea of a changed mind or repentance, but more on a felt level than on a cognitive level. The basic idea of **metamelomai** seems to be that of regret, a regret that may or may not lead one to turn to God. For example, Judas 'felt remorse' (**metamelomai**) for his betrayal of Jesus but he did not repent (Matt. 27:3). It is important to point out that many use Judas' account to prove that repentance is not part of saving faith. They say, 'Look at Judas, he "repented" (KJV), but he obviously did not become a Christian.' However, the word is not **metanoeo** (repent), but **metamelomai** (regret). Judas was sorrowful over his actions — things did not turn out as he had hoped. But he was not repentant — he did not turn from his sin to God for forgiveness. Neither was he converted (**epistrepho**) in the sense of turning to God. He simply felt remorse.

In 2 Corinthians 7:8,9 the distinction is clear. Paul wrote, 'For though I caused you sorrow by my letter, I do not regret it (**metamelomai**); though I did regret it (**metamelomai**) — for I see that that letter caused you sorrow, though only for a while — I now rejoice, not that you were made sorrowful, but that you were made sorrowful to the point of repentance (**metanoia**).'

True repentance may include the elements of regret and remorse and most likely will, but strictly speaking, repentance is a change of mind about something.

Repentance

The most important verb in our study is the Greek word **metanoeo**. This is the word most often translated 'repent' in the New Testament. In secular use it meant to change one's mind about something — what that something was depended on the context. In New Testament use, as we will see, **metanoeo** always has a reference to changing one's mind about sin in such a manner that the individual actually turns from sin.

Repentance in the Old Testament

A number of words in the Old Testament records are either translated or carry the meaning of 'repent' or 'repentance'. Walter Kaiser writes that 'the earliest prophetic use of the term to "repent", to "return" to the Lord, appears in 1 Samuel 7:3.'[12]

> Then Samuel spoke to all the house of Israel, saying, "If you return to the Lord with all your heart, remove the foreign gods and the Ashtaroth from among you and direct your hearts to the Lord and serve Him alone; and He will deliver you from the hand of the Philistines."

Notice that Samuel calls for the people not only to turn to God but to also turn from their idols. This is the typical Old Testament understanding of the concept of repentance and the constant message of the prophets, 'The Lord warned Israel and Judah, through all his prophets and every seer, saying, "Turn from your evil ways and keep My commandment"' (2 Kings 17:13). Old Testament repentance involved turning from sin and turning to God. This theme is carried over to the New Testament and is the constant and consistent message there as well.

Repentance in the New Testament

Before we explore the meaning and use of repentance in the New Testament we should first examine the favourite passage of those who deny that repentance has a place in the moment of salvation. In Acts 16 we have the account of the Philippian jailer who, due to a powerful display of God, asks Paul and Silas, 'Sirs, what must I do to be saved? Their reply, Believe in the Lord Jesus, and you shall be saved' (vv. 30,31). Since Paul said 'believe' and did not mention repentance or turning from sin to God, the conclusion is that repentance is an unnecessary act, indeed it is the addition of works for salvation. Had repentance been necessary Paul would have said so. Case closed!

But not so fast. Agreed, salvation is through faith alone in Christ alone, but there are a number of issues we need to investigate here. This simple answer by Paul, 'Believe in the Lord Jesus, and you shall be saved,' should raise a number of questions: What does he mean by believe? Who is the Lord Jesus? What does he mean by saved? The jailer wanted to be saved, but saved from what?

Salvation means 'rescue' or 'deliverance'. We can assume that the jailer wanted to be saved from his sin and its consequences. Implicitly, if not explicitly, this is repentance. But more germane to this discussion is what additional information concerning the gospel had been supplied. It is true that Paul did not mention repentance, but it is also true that he did not mention grace, the cross, the resurrection, the substitutionary death of Christ, and many more aspects of the gospel message. Does this mean these subjects are unrelated and unnecessary? Practically speaking I could walk up to any unbeliever and say, 'Believe on the Lord Jesus' and they could claim faith in Christ. But without more information they wouldn't even know who Christ is or what he had done. They might 'believe' but they are not saved.

Surely in our evangelistic efforts we would not ask someone to believe in Christ without first explaining the full gospel — and neither did Paul. In the very next verse we are told, 'And they spoke the word of the Lord to him' (v. 32). We don't know the content of this instruction but we can be confident that before the jailer truly placed faith in Christ he knew the gospel from beginning to end.

The point is that it is very difficult, and just plain wrong, to build a doctrine on a single passage, such as this one, in which we do not know exactly what was said.

On the other hand, while we don't know what details were given the jailer, we do know the contents of some apostolic sermons. At Pentecost, Peter's first sermon concluded with this invitation, 'Repent, and let each of you be baptized in the name of Jesus Christ for the forgiveness of your sins; and you shall receive the gift of the Holy Spirit' (Acts 2:38). Peter didn't misspeak; at his next opportunity he demanded, 'Repent therefore and return, that your sins may be wiped away' (Acts 3:19). Nor is this just a doctrine from the lips of Peter. Paul proclaims at the Areopagus, 'God is now declaring to men that all everywhere should repent' (Acts 17:30). Later when Paul was defending his apostolic commission to King Agrippa he explains that the Lord had sent him 'to open their (Gentiles) eyes so that they may turn from darkness to light and from the dominion of Satan to God, in order that they may receive forgiveness of sins and an inheritance among those who have been sanctified by faith in Me (Christ)' (Acts 26:18). The gospel that Paul preached called for men to turn (**epistrepho)**, by faith, from darkness to light and from the dominion of Satan to God's. Now, before we start arguing about what this means, all we have to do is drop to verses 19 and 20 and see what Paul thought it meant. 'I did not prove disobedient to the heavenly vision, but kept declaring both to those of Damascus first, and also at Jerusalem and then throughout all the region of Judea, and even to the Gentiles, that they should repent (**metanoeo**) and turn (**epistrepho**) to God, performing deeds appropriate to repentance.' Without question Paul saw his ministry as one of calling men and women to repent and turn to God which resulted in a transformed life.

But what does repentance mean?

Surely none can disagree with the clear words of Scripture. So what's the problem? The debate lies largely in the area of definition. The most important Greek word for repentance (**metanoeo**) means to change one's mind about something. Charles Ryrie and those like him teach that repentance is a changing of one's mind about who Jesus Christ is. Repentance, in their understanding, has nothing to do with sin. To change our minds about Christ is part of saving faith, but to change our minds about sin and its mastery over our lives is 'works', or so they say. Is this true? Does repentance have no reference to sin? Well, the only way to find out is to study Scripture itself.

By examining the use of the verb 'repent' (**metanoeo**) and the noun 'repentance' (**metanoia**) we should be able to determine how the word was used in the New Testament. Not every reference we will examine will be in the context of salvation or the gospel, for it is not our intention at this point to couple repentance with saving faith (we will do that later). At this point we simply want to see how the New Testament writers used the words **metanoeo/metanoia.** When the original readers of the New Testament encountered the word 'repent' what did they believe it meant?

Metanoeo and metanoia in the Gospels

Earlier I pointed out the Old Testament concept of repentance (and conversion). It is beyond doubt that when the Old Testament prophets called for repentance they were calling for the people to turn from their sins. The idea of 'changing their mind' about Christ would be completely foreign to the Old Testament writers. This should be kept in mind as we move into the Gospels. When John the Baptist and Jesus came preaching repentance what would their audience have understood them to mean? Surely the first thing to cross their minds would be to repent of sin and turn to God. Unless John, Jesus or the writers of the Gospels specifically redefined repentance in other terms we would expect repentance to carry the same connotation that it had for centuries. But we don't see any such change.

In the New Testament the meaning for **metanoeo/metanoia** is not defined by context in numerous passages. In other words, the words themselves are used but their specific meaning is debatable (Matt. 3:2; 3:8,11; 4:17; Mark 1:15; Luke 3:8; 16:30). As an example, John the Baptist calls for the people to 'repent for the kingdom of heaven is at hand' (Matt. 3:2). Jesus had not yet come on the scene when John uttered these words, so we would expect that the Jewish people would view them the same way they would have viewed similar messages from the Old Testament prophets, i.e. turn from sin and turn to God. Giving the benefit of the doubt we can't prove that is what John meant.

Conversely, in many other cases the context in which **meta-noeo/metanoia** is used the subject is clearly sin and the need to turn from it (Matt. 9:13; 11:20; 12:41; Mark 1:4; 2:17; Luke 3:3; 5:32; 6:12; 10:13; 11:32; 13:3,5; 15:7,10; 17:3). Some representative passages read: 'I tell you that in the same way, there will be more joy in heaven over one sinner who repents, than over ninety-nine righteous persons who need no repentance' (Luke 15:7); 'In the same way, I tell you, there is joy in the presence of the angels of God over one sinner who repents (Luke 15:10); 'If your brother sins, rebuke him; and if he repents, forgive him. And if he sins against you seven times a day, and returns to you seven times, saying, "I repent," forgive him' (Luke 17:3,4). At the Great Commission Jesus informs his disciples 'that repentance for forgiveness of sins should be proclaimed in His name to all the nations' (Luke 24:47). In each of these cases it is irrefutable that repent/repentance means changing one's mind or turning from sin. Not once is repentance defined as a changing of one's mind about Jesus.

Metanoeo and metanoia in the Acts

As Jesus leaves the scene we find the apostles, in obedience to the Great Commission, preaching repentance. Of the eleven uses of **metanoeo/metanoia** in the book of Acts, two (5:31; 8:22) are in the context of sin in general. Speaking to Simon the magician, for example, who claimed to be a believer but had committed a great sin, Peter says, 'Repent of this wickedness of yours, and pray the Lord, if possible, the intention of your heart may be forgiven you' (Acts 8:22). Simon must turn from his sin if he is to be forgiven.

In Acts 11:18; 13:24; 19:4 the contexts are not specific enough to dogmatically determine that repentance means a turning from sin, although this would be the most likely conclusion in each case.

The other five references are all in the context of salvation. We have seen some of these before but note carefully each context. In Acts 2:38 the Jews are told to repent for the forgiveness of sin. In Acts 3:19 they are to repent that their sins would be wiped away. Acts 17:30 says that God is calling men everywhere to repent. In Acts 20:21 Paul said that he preached to both Jews and Greeks the need for 'repentance toward God and faith in our Lord Jesus Christ'. Acts 26:20 is Paul's mission statement which is to call men to repent and turn to God. In none of these instances is repentance redefined as a changing of one's mind about who Jesus is. In at least three cases **metanoeo/metanoia** is definitely in the context of sin and forgiveness of sin. Our conclusion throughout the book of Acts is that nothing has changed — repentance still means what it has always meant — turning from sin.

Metanoeo and metanoia in Revelation

Every mention of **metanoeo/metanoia** in Revelation is in the immediate context of sin (2:5,16,21,22; 3:3,19; 9:20,21; 16:19,11). Revelation 2:21 reads, 'And I gave her time to repent; and she does not want to repent of her immorality. Revelation 9:21 reads as such, And they did not repent of their murders nor of their sorceries nor of their immorality nor of their thefts.' This is instructive since Revelation is the last New Testament book written and we find that the meaning of repentance has remained constant. In every clearly defined passage in the New Testament repentance has always meant a turning from sin. **Metanoeo/metanoia** is not always used in reference to salvation but it always carries the connotation of turning from sin.

Metanoeo and metanoia in the Epistles

In the epistles **metanoia** is found a number of times. Occasionally its meaning is indeterminate (Rom. 2:4; 2 Tim. 2:25; Heb. 6:1, 6). At other times sin is indisputably the context (2 Cor. 7:9, 10; Heb. 12:17). The only use of **metanoeo** in the epistles is 2 Corinthians

12:21, 'I am afraid that when I come again my God may humiliate me before you, and I may mourn over many of those who have sinned in the past, and not repented of the impurity, immorality and sensuality which they have practiced.' Here, once again, repentance is used in the context of sin. Never once have we found otherwise. Never once have we found repentance to have any reference to changing our minds about who Christ is. The context, when it can be determined, is always in the sphere of sin; in no passage is the idea of turning from sin foreign to the context.

With this in mind 2 Peter 3:9 should be pondered carefully, 'The Lord is not slow about His promise, as some count slowness, but is patient toward you, not wishing for any to perish but for all to come to repentance (metanoia).' If, when the Scriptures call us to repentance, it means turning from sin and turning to God as we have demonstrated, then to tell sinners that they do not have to turn from sin (they must only change their mind about Christ in order to be saved) is a false gospel. Salvation is through faith alone. Saving faith means that we have turned from our idols and sin in which we have trusted and long been enslaved, and turned to Christ by faith, in order to receive forgiveness and freedom from those sins (Rom. 6:12-14) and the righteousness of God (2 Cor. 5:21). To be saved surely means we are saved from something and to something. We are saved from sin and to righteousness found in Christ.

However, the opponents of repentance are quick to note that **metanoeo/metanoia** is seldom used in reference to salvation in the epistles. Therefore, they conclude, it is not part of the gospel. How do we refute this? A number of ways:

1) The book of Acts records the same time period during which many of the epistles were being written. For example when Paul spoke the words recorded in Acts 26:20 saying that his ministry has been one of calling people to 'repent and turn to God', he had already written 1 and 2 Thessalonians, 1 and 2 Corinthians, Galatians, and most likely, Romans. While he mentions repentance only four times in those five epistles, he nevertheless proclaims in Acts 26:18-20 that calling men and women to repentance has been his ministry all along.

2) *The New International Dictionary of New Testament Theology* has an excellent comment on this point,

> The fact that this group of words does not occur often in the Pauline writings (only 5 times) and not at all in the Johannine (apart from Revelation), does not mean that the idea of conversion is not present there but only that in the meantime a more specialized terminology had developed. Both Paul and John convey the idea of conversion by that of faith. Paul speaks of faith as 'being in Christ', as the 'dying and rising of a man with Christ', as the 'new creation', as 'putting on the new man'. The Johannine literature represents the new life in Christ as 'new birth', as a passing from death to life and from darkness to light, or as the victory of truth over falsehood and of love over hate.[13]

3) Since Scripture never contradicts Scripture it is a dangerous precedent to pit one portion of Scripture against another. We must recognize contextual distinctions, but to dismiss a clearly taught biblical doctrine because it is not found in certain pet passages is a serious error. For example, our Lord never once used the word 'grace' (and it is only found four times in the four Gospels, and never used in John's first epistle) yet who would dismiss it from its place of prominence in the gospel message? It is possible to over-compartmentalize the Scriptures. Yes, it is true that the epistles are written primarily to teach church age doctrine — but that does not mean that doctrine cannot be found in other portions of Scripture. Repentance, defined as turning from sin as part of saving faith, is clearly taught in many Scriptures. Who are we to redefine this word, or eliminate it altogether, because it is not found in passages in which some say it must be found (such as John's Gospel).

Word studies

Actually the burden of proof is on those who must wrestle with the clear calls for repentance found in Scripture (e.g. Acts 2:38; 3:19; 26:18,20). There are really only three options when the evidence is examined: Peter and Paul knew what they were talking about and were calling on people by faith to turn from their sins and turn to God. Or, these men and others were in error in what they taught (an unthinkable position). Or, repentance means something else, i.e. to change one's mind about whom Jesus is. Which is it?

We believe we have shown conclusive proof that in every case, where its meaning can be determined, **metanoeo/metanoia** in the New Testament means to turn from sin. On the other hand, there is not one clear use of any word for repentance that specifically and exclusively means to change one's mind about Christ. Not one!

Let's press on and examine the definitions given by word-study experts:

Wuest's Word Studies: Repentance in the New Testament 'includes not only the act of changing one's attitude towards an opinion of sin but also that of forsaking it...The act of repentance is based first of all and primarily upon an intellectual apprehension of the character of sin, man's guilt with respect to it, and man's duty to turn away from it.'[14]

Vines: 'In the NT the subject chiefly has reference to "repentance" from sin, and this change of mind involves both a turning from sin and a turning to God.'[15]

The New International Dictionary of New Testament Theology: 'Turning [in the OT] means giving a completely new direction to the man as a whole and a return to God. This includes turning away from evil...[In the NT] the predominantly intellectual understanding of **metanoia** as change of mind plays very little part in the NT. Rather the decision by the whole man to turn around is stressed. It is clear that we are concerned neither with a purely outward turning nor with a merely intellectual change of ideas.'[16]

Kittel: Repentance is a 'radical conversion, a transformation of nature, a definitive turning from evil, a resolute turning to God in total obedience.'

Conclusion

Some have concluded that to include repentance as part of saving faith is 'work-righteousness'. That is, it is an act that man must add to faith in order to be saved. We have shown from Scripture that such is not the case. Further, according to Scripture, repentance is a *gift* from God (see Acts 11:18; 2 Tim. 2:25). Just as no one would trust in Christ for salvation unless God enabled him to do so, so no one would repent if God did not grant him repentance. Repentance is not a work any more than faith is. The point is, when a person truly turns to Christ he also turns from sin. This is the clear teaching of the Word of God.

Notes

Introduction

1. Erwin Lutzer, *Exploding the Myths That Could Destroy America* (Chicago: Moody Press, 1986), p.203

Chapter 1 - A New Kind of Church

1. Richard Cimino and Don Lattin, 'Choosing My Religion', *American Demographics*, April 1999, pp.60-65
2. Ibid., p.62
3. Ibid., p.62
4. Ibid., p.63
5. Ibid., p.62
6. Ibid., p.62
7. Christian A. Schwarz, *The ABC's of Natural Church Development* (Carol Stream, Ill.: Church Smart Resources, 1998), p. 14.
8. Ibid., p.23
9. Ibid., p.14
10. John F. MacArthur, Jr., *Reckless Faith* (Wheaton: Crossway Books, 1994), p.52

Chapter 2 - Entertainment

1. Neal Gabler, *Life the Movie* (New York: Alfred A. Knopf, 1999), p.20
2. Neal Postman, *Amusing Ourselves to Death* (New York: Viking Press), p.77
3. Gabler, *Life the Movie*, p.16

4. Postman, *Amusing Ourselves to Death*, p.80,87
5. Ibid., p.47
6. Ibid., p.142
7. Ibid., p.146,148
8. Ibid., p.24
9. Don Myers, *All God's Children and Blue Suede Shoes*, as quoted in Mark Devries, *Family-Based Youth Ministry* (Downers Grove: InterVarsity Press, 1994), p.144
10. Gabler, *Life the Movie*, p.120
11. Ibid., p.197
12. Stephen R. Covey, *The Seven Habits of Highly Effective People* (New York: Simon & Schuster, Fireside, 1990), pp.18-19
13. As documented by Os Guinness, *A Time for Truth* (Grand Rapids: Baker Books, 2000), p.25
14. Postman, *Amusing Ourselves to Death*, p.121,124
15. Ibid., p.163
16. Guinness, *A Time for Truth*, p.34

Chapter 3 - Marken-Driven Philosophy

1. Rick Warren, *The Purpose-Driven Church* (Grand Rapids, Mich.: Zondervan, 1995), p.48
2. George Barna, *A Step-by-Step Guide to Church Marketing* (Ventura: Regal Books, 1992), pp.13,14
3. Ibid., p.19
4. Ibid., p.21
5. David F. Wells, *Losing Our Virtue* (Grand Rapids, Mich.: Eerdmans, 1998), p.180
6. Lee Strobel, *Inside the Mind of Unchurched Harry and Mary* (Grand Rapids: Zondervan, 1993), p.168
7. Barna, *Step-by-Step Guide to Church Marketing*, p.15
8. Ibid., 20,23,77
9. Ibid., p.23
10. Ibid. p.23
11. Ibid., p.21
12. Strobel, *Inside the Mind of Unchurched Harry and Mary*, p.56
13. Ibid., p.50

14. Ibid., p.57
15. Ibid., p.56
16. Ibid., pp.58,59
17. Ibid., p.76
18. Ibid., pp.213-214
19. David F. Wells, *God in the Wasteland* (Grand Rapids: Eerdmans, 1994), p.78
20. It was close to 50 percent in the late 1950s and 43 percent in 1999. See Jody Veenker, 'Culture Clash', *Christianity Today*, 10 July 2000, p. 20.
21. Wells, *God in the Wasteland*, p.79
22. George Barna, *A Step-by-Step Guide to Church Marketing*, p.170
23. As documented by Os Guinness, *Dining with the Devil* (Grand Rapids: Baker Book House, 1994), p.38
24. Wells, *God in the Wasteland*, p.82
25. Guinness, *Dining with the Devil*, p.59
26. Ibid., p.63
27. Ibid., p.27
28. Ibid., pp.30,31
29. Michael S. Horton, 'Recovering the Plumb Line', in *The Coming Evangelical Crisis*, ed. John H. Armstrong (Chicago: Moody Press, 1996), p.254
30. Wells, *Losing Our Virtue*, p.202

Chapter 4 - Psychology
1. Guinness, *A Time for Truth*, p.43
2. Warren, p.197ff
3. Ibid., p.219
4. Ibid., p.139
5. Ibid., p.220
6. See Ibid., pp.197ff
7. Ibid., p.295
8. Guinness, *Dining with the Devil*, 1994, p.84
9. *Christianity Today*, May 17, 1993, p.31
10. *Time for Truth*, p.78

Chapter 5 - A Church With The Wrong Foundation

1. Wells, *Losing Our Virtue*, p.32
2. As quoted in G.A. Pritchard, *Willow Creek Seeker Services* (Grand Rapids, MI: Baker Book House, 1998), p.51
3. Ibid., p.53
4. Strobel, pp.214-215
5. Pritchard, pp.70-73
6. Ibid., p.143
7. Ibid., p.177
8. R. Albert Mohler Jr., 'Evangelical: What's in a Name?' in *The Coming Evangelical Crisis*, ed. John H. Armstrong (Chicago: Moody Press, 1996), p.40
9. Wells, *God in the Wasteland*, p.76
10. Wells, *Losing Our Virtue*, p.197
11. 'In the Name of God' video with Peter Jennings.
12. Wells, *Losing Our Virtue*, p.40.
13. Pritchard, p.233
14. Ibid., pp.227,235
15. Ibid., p.234
16. Pritchard, pp.238-239 (Percentages of Christians and non-Christians attending Willow Creek are estimates based upon the author's research.).
17. Ibid., p.200,207
18. Ibid., p.244.
19. Wells, *Losing Our Virture*, p.199,205
20. Ibid., p.209

Chapter 6 - A Church With The Wrong Message

1. Horton, 'Recovering the Plumb Line', p.256
2. Strobel, *Inside the Mind of Unchurched Harry and Mary*, p.45
3. Ibid., p.80
4. Ibid., p.58
5. Ibid., p.47
6. MacArthur, Jr., *Reckless Faith*, p.52
7. Strobel, p.50

8. Ibid., p.56
9. Ibid., p.59
10. Wells, *Losing Our Virtue*, p.207
11. Guinness, *Time for Truth*, p.78
12. Strobel, p.57
13. Ibid.
14. Wells, *Losing Our Virtue*, p.107
15. Strobel, p.71 (emphasis in the original)
16. Ibid., p.92
17. Ibid., p.124 (emphasis in the original)
18. Wayne Jacobsen, 'The Numbers Game: A Threat to Churches Large and Small', *Leadership* 4, no. 1 (winter 1983): p.50
19. Pritchard, p.250
20. Ibid., p.254-256
21. Ibid., p.260
22. Ibid., p.260
23. John MacArthur Jr., *Ashamed of the Gospel* (Wheaton: Crossway Books, 1994), p.24
24. As quoted by G.A. Pritchard, p.316.
25. MacArthur, Jr., *Ashamed of the Gospel*, pp.72,111,128
26. As quoted by MacArthur, *Ashamed of the Gospel*, p.67
27. Wells, *Losing Our Virtue*, p.207

Chapter 7 - A Church Focused On The Wrong Need

1. Michael S. Hamilton, 'The Triumph of the Praise Songs: How Guitars Beat Out the Organ in the Worship Wars', *Christianity Today*, July 12, 1999, p.30
2. Ibid.
3. Guinness, *Dining with the Devil*, p.27
4. Wells, *Losing Our Virtue*, p.40
5. As quoted by J. P. Moreland, *Love Your God with All Your Mind* (Colorado Springs: NavPress, 1997), p.19
6. William James, *The Varieties of Religious Experience* (New York: Longmans, Green, and Co., 1922), p.506
7. Donald G. Bloesch, 'Whatever Happened to God?', *Christianity Today*, 5 February, 2001, p.55

8. Schwarz, *The ABC's of Natural Church Development*, p.14
9. Michael Horton, ed., *The Agony of Deceit* (Chicago: Moody Press, 1990), pp.163,164

Chapter 8 - How Then Shall We Preach?

1. Bloesch, 'Whatever Happened to God?' p.54
2. John MacArthur Jr., 'How Shall We Then Worship?' in *The Coming Evangelical Crisis*, ed. John H. Armstrong (Chicago: Moody Press, 1996), p.176
3. MacArthur, *Ashamed of the Gospel*, p.72
4. Guinness, *Time for Truth*, p.52
5. Bill Hull, *Power Religion – The Selling Out of the Evangelical Church* (Chicago: Moody Bible Institute, 1992)
6. John F. MacArthur, Jr., *Pastoral Ministry*, (Dallas: Word, 1995), p.253
7. John Piper, *The Supremacy of God in Preaching* (Grand Rapids: Baker Books, 1990), pp.9-11,30,109
8. MacArthur, *Pastoral Ministry*, p.260

Chapter 9 - How Then Shall We Sing?

1. MacArthur, *The Coming Evangelical Crisis,* pp.182-183.
2. Leonard Payton, 'How Shall We Then Sing?' in *The Coming Evangelical Crisis*, ed. John H. Armstrong (Chicago: Moody Press, 1996), p.194.
3. Paul Anderson, 'Balancing Form and Freedom', *Leadership* 7, no. 2 (spring 1996): 32.
4. Timothy Dudley Smith, 'Why Wesley Still Dominates Our Hymnbook', p.11, and William J. Reynolds, 'Three Hymnals That Shaped Today's Worship', p.36, *Christian History* 10, no. 3 (31).
5. Ibid., pp.20,36.
6. Kenneth W. Osbeck, *101 Hymn Stories* (Grand Rapids, Mich.: Kregel, 1982), pp. 35,36.
7. Wells, *Losing Our Virtue*, p.44.
8. Payton, 'How Shall We Then Sing?' p.191.
9. Ibid., p.194.

10. Ibid., p. 203.

Chapter 10 - The Gospel According To Warren

1. John MacArthur, Jr., *Hard to Believe*, (Nashville: Thomas Nelson Publishers, 2003), p.12
2. Ibid., p.13

Chapter 11 - A Church At The Crossroad

1. Benjamin B. Warfield, *Selected Shorter Writings*, vol. 1 (Nutley: Presbyterian and Reformed, 1970), p.47
2. Ibid., p.49

Appendix - Repentance

1. Charles Spurgeon, *Metropolitan Tabernacle Pulpit* Vol. 11, (Banner of Truth 1992), p.138.
2. As quoted in *The Day Drawing Near*, Vol. 2 #2, p. 4.
3. A. W. Tozer, *Man: The Dwelling Place of God* (Harrisburg: Christian Publications, 1966), p.143
4. A. W Tozer, *The Root of Righteous* (Harrisburg: Christian Publications 1955), p.85
5. Benjamin B. Warfield, *Biblical and Theological Studies* (Presbyterian & Reformed, 1952), p.403
6. J. I. Packer, *Evangelism and the Sovereignty of God* (Downers Grove: Inter-Varsity Press, 1961), p.72
7. The Westminster Shorter Catechism section LXXXVII.
8. See Charles Ryrie, *So Great Salvation* (Chicago: Moody Press, 1997), pp.96-99
9. See Zane Hodges, *The Gospel Under Siege* (Dallas: Redencoin Viva, 1981)
10. William Barclay, *Turning to God* (Philadelphia: The Westminster Press, 1964), p.20
11. Colin Brown (General Editor), *The New International Dictionary of New Testament Theology*, Vol. 1 (Grand Rapids: Zondervan, 1979), p.355

12. Walter C. Kaiser, Jr., *Toward an Old Testament Theology* (Grand Rapids: Academie Books, 1978), p.137

13. Ibid., p. 359.

14. Kenneth Wuest, *Studies in the Vocabulary of the Greek New Testament* (Grand Rapids: Wm. B. Eerdmans, 1976), p.28

15. *Vines Complete Expository Dictionary of Old and New Testament Words* (Nashville: Thomas Nelson, 1985), p.525

16. Gerhard Kittle, *Theological Dictionary of the New Testament* (Grand Rapids: Eerdmans, 1985), pp.1002-1003

Coming soon from Evangelical Press...

This little church
STAYED AT HOME

Many churches, riding the faddish waves of our times, have gone 'to market', but not all. Some churches are trying to 'stay home', that is, remain firmly grounded in the Scriptures. Still, the pressures mount, the temptations are repackaged, and the schemes of the devil become more and more persuasive.

In Dr. Gilley's forthcoming sequel, *This Little Church Stayed Home*, he explores the manifold temptations of conservative churches to sell out to modern trends and innovations. Churches parleying with 'new measures' will be challenged to remain true to the historic doctrines of the Christian faith and to remain faithful to God's chosen means of converting sinners to himself — the good news of Jesus Christ.

Pastors, seminary students, church leaders, and Christians who want God's Word to be paramount in their lives will find *This Little Church Stayed Home* a timely message to a Christian subculture fixated on marketing the glorious gospel of Jesus Christ.

ISBN: 0 85234 603 4

113223

A wide range of excellent books on spiritual subjects is available from Evangelical Press. Please write to us for your free catalogue or contact us by e-mail. Full details are also available on our web site.

Evangelical Press
Faverdale North Industrial Estate, Darlington, Co. Durham, DL3 0PH, England

Evangelical Press USA
P. O. Box 825, Webster, New York 14580, USA

e-mail: sales@evangelicalpress.org

web: http://www.evangelicalpress.org